# JIMMY McGOVERN'S CRACKER

# FROM TRAGEDY TO SUCCESS -
# A NOIR OF THE NINETIES

## Josephine M. Dunn

# PREFACE

In 1993 a remarkable television series *Cracker* was aired in the UK. Inspired by Jacobean tragedy, influenced by Film Noir, written by Jimmy McGovern & crafted by a team at Granada TV.

"I didn't want him. The character I had in mind was a wee bit like me at the time, a thin wiry guy with energy to burn. The actor I had in mind was John Cassavettes, a wonderful actor and great filmmaker, with a crackling sense of energy. So we went to meet Robbie, and I said: 'Sorry, I see him as a thin man and you're a fat bastard.' But he was great, he wanted it, he brought humanity. It was that, mainly. A big sweaty mess of a man." Jimmy McGovern *Variety online*, May 2017.

This book explores *Cracker*'s dramatic, literary roots & filmic roots showing how they shaped its narrative in story & style. The author examines historical contexts & conventions to explain why the time was right for a psychological thriller. By looking at mood & themes, stylistic features & techniques, particularly the use of light & shadow and the importance of water, the author shows how *Cracker* developed its dramatic impact.

This serious critical work is enlivened by many exclusive insights from the creative team who brought *Cracker* to life. The author interviewed writer Jimmy McGovern, the 3 directors, Michael Winterbottom, Andy Wilson & Simon Cellan-Jones, producer Gub Neal, cinematographer Ivan Strasberg, designer Chris Wilkinson & production executive Craig McNeil. The author draws on her 40 year career in film & television production & on a personal connection with actor Robbie Coltrane who was a near neighbour in Hackney during the 1980s.

# REVIEW

*A review by Robb Hart, British Producer & Director – responsible for the launch of MTV Europe, now working in California on Commercials.*

Josephine Dunn's writing examines one of the seminal TV shows of the 1990's, and gives it the position it deserves in the history not just of television but drama.

Her book embraces the history of drama by looking at the evolution of storytelling from the ancient Greeks through the Jacobean and Elizabethan periods, to film noir and films such as Silence of the Lambs.

The reverence that is usually reserved for the analysis of film is employed here on a TV series where through 25 episodes it established what has become a new genre of drama. Much like the significance of Lynch's Twin Peaks, Cracker can be seen as a pivotal development in television history. There would be no Dexter or even Game of Thrones without it.

Once it was unheard of for 'A' list actors to do TV, now the likes of Robert DeNiro and Dustin Hoffman are no longer just film actors. In this period of deconstruction as the network model hands over to the streaming phenomenon, the game changing TV shows that paved the way must include Cracker.

In this book the shifts of structure, the antecedents and the radical differences in traditional plot and character roles are examined with the forensic and psychoanalytic skills that echo Cracker's approach. Yet through the candid and very frank interviews with the key players, Josephine allows the story be told by the creators often in a charmingly honest manner.

> *Film Noir is also the source of much of the writing style, with McGovern freely admitting ,"I grew up on American films and they have influenced every aspect of my life and anybody my age who says they didn't is a liar. So there."*

Before Robbie Coltrane was Hagrid, and even before he was Cracker we was Josephine's neighbour. Before McGovern wrote Cracker he honed his craft in Brookside. The book chronicles the period leading to the early nineties that provided the context and influences that channeled into the creation of Cracker. There is a sense of first hand intimacy with the subject that gives the writing what could now be described as embedded journalism.

From Tragedy To Success - A Noir Of The Nineties, balances anecdotes about what happened behind the scenes, with the critical reaction, and rating success of the show. For anyone who is interested in how drama is created, what influences it's development and why we should look back on milestones like this series to understand not only how the influence television history, but were integrally part of the social history we grew up in.

# CONTENTS

# ILLUSTRATIONS & FIGURES

# INTRODUCTION

On 27th September 1993 a remarkable new television series began on ITV. Granada promoted *Cracker* as an "uncompromising and tough" series, a "detective drama with a difference, starring Robbie Coltrane as a dangerous but brilliant, wisecracking and sexy, Manchester-based clinical psychologist called Fitz." [1]

*Cracker*, with its leading protagonist the maverick criminal psychologist Fitz ( Eddie Fitzgerald), began at Granada with the germ of an idea for a new detective series following the success of Silence Of The Lambs. It was an attempt to create 'intelligent' television through the conscious construction of narrative; cops and robbers were out, psychology was in.

Even on first viewing it was obvious that *Cracker* was indeed a drama with a difference. It was a well crafted piece which demonstrated care and attention to detail in every way; from the complex narrative structure of parallel plots, witty dialogue and dynamic interplay between characters to sophisticated direction, atmospheric design and stylish photography and lighting. It was apparent that *Cracker* was not just another detective series but was informed by a number of literary, theatrical and filmic antecedents as well as its television predecessors. Some elements of *Cracker* , for instance, the parallel plot structure, seemed to come from a theatrical tradition, where two stories are not just interconnected, as the crime and domestic stories might be in a police drama, but actually mirror each other directly or ironically. This kind of structure is commonly found in Jacobean tragedy. Other elements of *Cracker*, for instance, the detective figure, the urban setting and the use of light as a digetic actant, seemed to stem from a strong film noir influence.

At first the combination might seem an unlikely one and yet critics, from the quality press to the tabloids, recognised these contributory factors and praised them. Many critics noted the quality of the writing, the pacy direction, the moody atmosphere. They found the stories had a gritty realism, the action gripping, the acting superb. Maureen Paton particularly

---

[1]   Press pack - Granada LWT International Ltd.

noted *Cracker's* , "moody Chandleresque style", [2] while Thomas Sutcliffe described the plot as "solidly constructed ... a sense of lives extending beyond the frame of the story," [3] Peter Barnard noted the "two stories" [4] and Peter Paterson found the "two parallel but apparently unconnected stories ... converged."[5] Even those who found the plot difficult to follow at first or who could not stomach the violence of murder scenes discovered that *Cracker* was compulsory viewing. Though their methods varied, Margaret Forwood encouraging readers gently to watch , "the most successful debut of the season," [6] while the Sun ordered its readers, "Don't miss this," [7] the message was the same. A fuller picture of the critical response to Cracker, and details of the awards it won, can be found in appendix 1.

The industry and audiences agreed, demonstrating their approval with awards and high and consistent viewing figures which increased as the series continued. The first episode of *Cracker* gained an audience of over ten million while audience figures rose to almost twelve million by episode seven, the last in series one. Series two figures averaged over thirteen million rising to almost fourteen million for series three. A fuller picture of audience figures and share, recorded by BARB, is given in fig. 2.

Producer, Gub Neal, initiated the idea, although he says "Jimmy (writer Jimmy McGovern) animated it and brought it to life and did all the things that make it work." [8] As a producer, Gub Neal feels that his role is "to bring the elements together". Having conceived the idea for the series he knew it needed a character in the centre who, in order for the narrative to work, subverts the genre and subverts the normal in terms of expectations". [9] At this stage Neal did not know how or what that might be but knew, at an emotional level, that it had to be. The character had to be "someone that was fundamentally dangerous and unpredictable and

---

[2] Daily Mirror, 5.10.93.
[3] The Independent, 28.9.93.
[4] The Times, 28.9.93.
[5] TV Mail Reviews, 28.9.93.
[6] Daily Express, 2.10.93.
[7] Sun TV, 4.10.93.
[8] Author's interview, Gub Neal - BBC TV Centre - 20.4.1994

at the same time embodied a certain heroic quality which I, you know, talking bluntly, you say there's something there that you actually admire and respect." [10]

Robert Lindsay was approached, but turned it down saying he did not want to play another character who was so hysterical because he had just done GBH (written by another Liverpool writer, Alan Bleasdale, for C4- Lindsay won a BAFTA for best actor) and did not want to get typecast. Jimmy had not begun writing at this point, although he had finally agreed to write the series, having initially turned it down several times. Neal sent the outline "such as it existed, that I had just concocted one afternoon in the office," [11] to Robbie Coltrane. "I had met him briefly about ten years ago," says Neal, "when I was organising a thing at the Donmar Warehouse for Band Aid (Actor Aid). Robbie turned up late and was fairly drunk and fairly abusive and all the rest of it. I remember very distinctly watching him. I was going out with this girl at the time and he started sort of mauling her in a way that was kind of dangerous but sort of harmless and I thought he's a very interesting person, because he's getting away with something which anybody else would not get away with and yet it's just politically incorrect. That expresses certain power. With Robbie there is something lurking there all the time, a sort of rift, a sense of danger, a sense of someone who isn't at ease with themselves." [12] Coltrane found it "interesting" but wanted to see a script. Jimmy, still unsure if he was going to be free to write the script, was completely against Coltrane playing the part, seeing the character of Fitz played by a John Cassavetes type. McGovern says, "I had this thin, wiry guy in mind but then I met Robbie and everything evolved from there." [13] In fact the first two episodes comprising the first story, The Mad Woman In The Attic, were written before their meeting. McGovern was surprised to find Coltrane had a brilliant mind and

---

[9] Author's interview, Gub Neal - BBC TV Centre - 20.4.1994
[10] Author's interview, Gub Neal - BBC TV Centre - 20.4.1994

[11] Author's interview, Gub Neal - BBC TV Centre - 20.4.1994

[12] Author's interview, Gub Neal – BBC TV Centre – 20.4.1994
[13] Author's interview, Jimmy McGovern – telephone – April 1994

"was Fitz in everything but size." Hostile at the time of meeting McGovern admits that he was worried he had been rude to Coltrane. Neal explains," he (Jimmy) got completely pissed and told him (Coltrane) he had seen him as a thin man. If we had got Stephen Rea to play the part it would have been too overcharged, too spiteful. Jimmy's writing has got a lot of piss and vinegar in it and you've got to find a way to make it more friendly, more accessible so that people don't turn off. Robbie offers the sense of someone who even if you didn't like them, you wanted to like them. You'd rather have him as your friend than as an enemy, like the big boy at school, if you're not his friend, you are subject to his abuse."[14]

Drinking to excess is something that McGovern and Coltrane share. An alcoholic and member of Gamblers Anonymous, McGovern puts much of his personal experience into his writing. Gambling and drinking, plus the resulting argumentative behaviour contribute directly to Fitz, other less obvious factors are demonstrated in other characters; the quiet, sympathetic portrayal of the priest, played by Adrian Dunbar, in The Mad Woman In The Attic , is only possible through McGovern's catholic upbringing, the basis of Sean in To Say I Love You springs from McGovern's own severe stutter - he writes, "up to the time I was thirty I was treated like shit by lots of people." [15] Coltrane's drinking has less easily identifiable roots. Coltrane's childhood was middle class but the strictness of his father , a police surgeon,  was in odd contrast to the artistic nature of his pianist mother, who invited a stream of bohemians to their house for soirees. This explains why Coltrane is an adequate artist, a graduate of Glasgow School of Art, passionate socialist, self taught intellectual and consummate mimic, but it is his size that has formed his character. [16] Neal says," Robbie's persona as a comic has been largely part of the Comedy of Cruelty - you can't be a fat comic and do nice humour because you are the butt of your own jokes - to some extent that's how comic convention works." [17]  Coltrane has worked all his

---

[14] Author's interview,  Gub Neal – BBC TV Centre – 20. 4 1994
[15] Letter to author from Jimmy McGovern – May 1994
[16] Robbie Coltrane's conversations with the author – Southborough Road, London E9 – 1985 - 1987
[17] Author's interview – Gub Neal – BBC TV Centre – 20.4.1994

life to create a personality that is larger than his physical bulk, like McGovern he has struggled to overcome a disability and it has become a pilgrimage. Both ultimately survivors, it is not surprising that their collaboration should produce such success: Broadcasting Press Guild Awards 1993 - Best Writer, Best Actor, Best Series; BAFTA 1994 - Best Writer, Best Actor, Best Photography; McGovern also winning The Whitbread Scousology Award - TV Personality 1994 - although it took the calculating and sometimes, I feel, dispassionate control of Neal to produce it.

It is a mark of *Cracker's* acceptance as part of contemporary culture that it has reached a point of recognition where it can be the subject of a current joke. "Q: What do you get if you cross Santa Claus with Robbie Coltrane ? A: A Christmas Cracker." [18] It is not unusual for a popular television series to receive recognition for the quality of its production, but what is remarkable is the textual complexity and richness of style in *Cracker*. I was determined to investigate whether this complexity and richness arose as a happy accident or as the culmination of ordered planning and informed imagination. Before beginning an academic study of *Cracker,* I interviewed a number of people instrumental in the making of the series. The producer, writer, directors, designer, cinematographer, script editor and others involved in the production of the first series of Cracker all gave exclusive and lengthy interviews which have informed this book. These interviews, along with profiles of the three directors, form Appendix 2. As they give an insight into 'the team' and explain their methods of working and attitudes to *Cracker,* readers may find it valuable to reference appendix 2 before reading the critical body of the book. Robbie Coltrane moved into a house in Southborough Road where I was living in 1985. Many conversations took place while he shared whisky with my husband, called into our house on the way to and from the local shops and enjoyed other social occasions with us. Sadly in the later years when researching this book Robbie was not available for further interviews, although several approaches were made

---

[18] Jim Bowen, Gag Tag, BBC1, 26.1.96

though his agent at the time.

It was not by chance *Cracker* took the form it had. As producer Gub Neal says," nothing in the plotting of the first series was co-incidental, nothing was down to luck, ....It's no good looking at Hollywood, Hollywood has no value. Hollywood films are entirely derived from traditions in English literature that are established and have been for centuries."[19] However, Neal's attitude to Hollywood did not stop him recommending writer Jimmy McGovern should look at *Double Indemnity* and *The Postman Always Rings Twice* in addition to the Jacobean tragedy *The Changeling*.

Since the producer himself suggested the possible influence of Jacobean tragedy and film noir it made perfect sense to embark on a close study of the two forms and make textual comparisons with *Cracker*. Through examination of written texts, film narratives and academic works I have found evidence that *Cracker's* plotting is based on models from popular Renaissance and Jacobean theatre, particularly on Jacobean tragedy. Classical tragedy also gives rise to Cracker's heroes, both tragic and ironic, directly and through its influence on Film Noir. The mood and tone of *Cracker* have direct roots in Film Noir, as does much of the style of the design and the lighting. Film Noir is also the source of much of the writing style, with McGovern freely admitting ,"I grew up on American films and they have influenced every aspect of my life and anybody my age who says they didn't is a liar. So there."

I believe the evidence is so strong that many people recognised it instinctively as part of their cultural inheritance although perhaps not able or honest enough to acknowledge it as McGovern does. I have examined the historical, political and social factors existing during the late sixteenth and early seventeenth centuries, the pre and post world war II era and made comparisons to today in order to establish why different times could give rise to similar forms of drama. What emerges is the fact that unsettled times have all given rise to forms of tragedy with a psychological slant. Following investigation into historical contexts and conventions I have made a close comparison of *Cracker* to dramatic forms belonging to the Jacobean era and the genre of film noir. Many similarities emerged and I also established that

---

[19]  Authors interview, 20.4.94.

Jacobean drama and film noir both draw strongly on their common history in Greek tragedy.

The decision to have an echoing narrative was part of a conscious decision at the outset. As producer Gub Neal says, "that's good plotting..... nothing in the plotting of the first series was co-incidental, nothing was down to luck....."[20]. There were structural decisions taken before writing began and Jimmy was able to hothouse the ideas he had for Cracker with two or three other people; Neal, and script editors Catriona McKenzie and Nicola Schindler, both Oxford graduates. They felt that storytelling in television did not have to be any more mundane than it already was. Neal says," television can either be completely banal and deal with the everyday and represent a kind of moral affirmation of expectations, values and so on, and to some extent that's what Lovejoy, Pie In The Sky, Morse and essentially generic television serials represent, or it can aim a bit higher by trying to create something which is more diverse and in a sense more complex, though not necessarily more complicated, in its range and also in terms of how it appeals to people." [21] Neal was very aware of trying to create a series which would appeal to "us" (the Oxbridge / Independent / Guardian reader) without losing the popular audience essential for the continued success of a programme.

Neal looked for role models for popular drama in Renaissance and Jacobean theatre where he found ,"a ripping good yarn layered with levels of complexity which are to do with something that appeals to the intellect, something that appeals to the emotions, baser instincts." [22] The reason these plays work is because they operate on a number of levels, they have resonating plots so that the personal life of the characters is affected, moved, changed by the events that unfold during the course of the story; the character which comes out at the end is different to that which went in at the beginning. Neal feels that, though it requires a huge amount of energy,

[20] Author's interview – Gub Neal – BBC TV Centre – 20.4.1994
[21] Author's interview – Gub Neal – BBC TV Centre 20.4.1994
[22] Author's interview – Gub Neal – BBC TV Centre – 20.4.1994

television drama could work in this way if only ," people applied themselves to television with the same degree of intelligence and the same degree of respect as writing novels, plays or talking on the radio".[23] He sees *Cracker* as a piece of Renaissance television which achieved success because of Granada's ability to take risks and Sally Head's (Head of Drama - Granada) willingness to encourage dangerous combinations.

So is *Cracker* entirely a product of the literary cognoscente, or should we consider in its authorship ALL the contributors to the construction of the narrative?

It would, of course, be folly to assume that there is one controlling factor influencing the television narrative since it is the sum of all messages emitted and received. In Rhetoric of the Image, Barthes discusses the need for shared codes, practical, national, cultural, aesthetic, in order to interpret signs in the 'correct' way. A body of knowledge or 'attitude' about, "tourism, housekeeping, knowledge of art - certain of which may obviously be lacking in this or that individual," [24] will affect the way in which an image is perceived. So, too, it is with television narrative. With its multiple authorship, television possesses the ability to contain many, often contradictory, messages even before it is received by viewers possessing different codes for interpretation.

Literary rules may apply to the conception and structure of *Cracker* but the continual references in the writing, performance and visual style of the series lie in Hollywood films of the forties and fifties, even the lighting belongs to the film noir / detective genre. So, while the 'ripping good yarn' that is the basic 'detective' story in *Cracker* is open to Proppian[25] analysis, one must consider the layered elements (filmic and cultural references, transtextual associations of actors etc) which resonate upwards and outwards from this parametrically. The reason why *Cracker* works, that it

---

[23] Author's interview – Gub Neal – BBC TV Centre – 20.4.1994
[24] Barthes, Roland, Image, Music, Text (London: Fontana Press, 1977. p47

13

has met with critcal acclaim and attracted a popular audience, is because it is not necessary to receive every indice or understand every reference in order to enjoy it. Like Jacobean theatre or literary works such as Alice in Wonderland the series operates on may levels and is therefore open to may interpretations. None of these interpretations is right or wrong, they naturally depend on the pre-programmed codes of the viewer who may see part of what the author intended, all of it or something entirely different. We must not forget that because television is subject to multiple authorship, the sum of its parts may very often exceed the individual components.

One has to accept that producer Gub Neal can state categorically, "It's no good looking at Hollywood, Hollywood has no value. Hollywood films are entirely derived from traditions in English literature that are established and have been for centuries,"[26] and yet Neal's attitude to Hollywood did not stop him recommending writer Jimmy McGovern should look at *Double Indemnity* and *The Postman Always Rings Twice* in addition to the Jacobean tragedy *The Changeling.*

Gub Neal suggested that McGovern look *at Double Indemnity, The Postman Always Rings Twice* and *The Changeling* when writing the second *Cracker* story. McGovern says," that theme of a man being egged on to destruction by a manipulative (now there's a sexist word) woman, well it's the oldest story in the world. It's Adam and Eve. So I reckon any writer would be attracted to it without *Double Indemnity* and *The Postman Always Rings Twice*. But I do love those two films (and the latter as a novel) so, yes, they must have had an influence even if only at a subconscious level. *The Changeling* didn't influence me one bit. I found it interesting that Gub recommended it. Television is full of people with English Literature backgrounds and Oxbridge ties. That, I reckon, is why our films are so crap."[27] You can almost hear Jimmy's placement of inverted commas around 'interesting' when he refers to the Jacobean century Thomas

---

[25] Propp, Vladimir, Morphology of the Folktale, (University of Texas Press, 1968)
[26] Authors interview, 20.4.94.
[27] Jimmy McGovern's letter to the author – May 1994

Middleton / Rowley play *The Changeling*. It is also relevant to note that McGovern refers to the films of *Double Indemnity* and *Postman Always Rings Twice* before the novels by James M. Cain. *Double Indemnity* (Paramount - 1944) is described as 'a seminal work in the emergence of film noir as an explosive movement in American film." [28] The short novel by Cain was based on the notorious Snyder Gray case of 1927 and the screenplay written by Raymond Chandler and Billy Wilder, who also directed the film. Cain, born in Annapolis, USA in 1892, began as a journalist but became a bestselling author in 1934 with the publication of his first and most famous novel *The Postman Always Rings Twice*. This was made as a film by MGM in 1946 with Lana Turner's steamy performance as Cora Smith undiminished by the censors cuts. The remake, in 1980, with Jack Nicholson and Jessica Lange is far less suggestive, despite overt sexuality on the kitchen table and, like the television remakes of *Double Indemnity* in 1954 and 1973, fails to live up to the original. Co-incidentally, Cain had a family background similar to Robbie Coltrane, in that he had an academic (professor) father and musical (opera singer) mother.

Jimmy McGovern not only has a great love of Hollywood, his writing style is imbued by the detective films he escaped into as a child. For those not familiar with Cain as a writer, he has a style similar, if a little cruder than Chandler. Perhaps, Chandler, following after Cain, was able to perfect the older man's style. Both, however, share a journalistic or documentary clipped commentary style. Chandler, in his first studio assignment *Double Indemnity*, was able to add his own distinctive brand of cynicism whilst keeping much of the original dialogue of the novel. McGovern, too, has a direct way of writing with the capacity to make any experience with a group of characters felt rather than observed. The viewer is charged with emotion and forced into a relationship with those people, mostly an actively uncomfortable one. The audience is put into situations they would not normally find themselves in and made to participate. There is a fatality about Cain's writing which also surfaces in McGovern, again often to do with his Liverpool Irish working class catholic upbringing. McGovern says," I grew

---

[28] 2nd Virgin Film Guide 1993

up during the reign of Pope Pius 12th. He was fiercely opposed (like this Polish misogynist we've got now) to birth control and people reckon it was his influence that led to the birth of so many babies. Bollocks. It was Clark Gable. Clark's eyes would twinkle; next minute it's moonlight on the beach and orgasmic waves crashing in. Clark never fumbled for a johnny or got his underpants caught round his ankles so woe betide any man who did." [29] What is forbidden is therefore what is most exciting. Sex is what it is to do with, both in Cain's books and McGovern's screenplays; passion is the driving force behind the main characters, ranging from violent outward display of feelings to the twisted result of the suppression of desire.

In Cain's books, we know immediately that Sex will lead to trouble. In *The Postman Always Rings Twice* we are introduced to Cora, "she had a sulky look to her, and her lips stuck out in a way that made me want to mash them in for her."[30] In *Double Indemnity* Huff meets Phyllis for the first time and ," all of a sudden she looked at me, and I felt a chill creep straight up my back and into the roots of my hair." [31] There is no mistaking the effect these women have on Cain's male characters, and much of this mans willingness to do or die for love (sex) is evoked in McGovern's writing.

I believe the evidence is so strong that many people recognised it instinctively as part of their cultural inheritance although perhaps not able or honest enough to acknowledge it as McGovern does. I have examined the historical, political and social factors existing during the late sixteenth and early seventeenth centuries, the pre and post world war II era and made comparisons to today in order to establish why different times could give rise to similar forms of drama. What emerges is the fact that unsettled times have all given rise to forms of tragedy with a psychological slant. Following investigation into historical contexts and conventions I have made a close comparison of *Cracker* to dramatic forms belonging to the Jacobean era and the genre of film noir. Many similarities emerged, and I also established that Jacobean drama and film noir both draw strongly on their common history in

---

[29] Jimmy McGovern's letter to the author – May 1994
[30] Cain, James M., The Postman Always Rings Twice (Bath: Chivers Press, 1985) p11
[31] Cain, James M., Double Indemnity and The Embezzler (London: Robert Hale Ltd., 1986) p4

Greek tragedy.

As I will show that *Cracker* is a contemporary tragedy and certainly not just 'another detective series', I now include some definitions of tragedy to demonstrate what the form is and why it exists.

> All narrative foregrounds problems - comedy moves towards final reconciliation, tragedy is subject to no such imperative, tragedy is a point of departure.[32]

> Tragedy, the form of drama responsible for interpreting to man the conditions of his own being.[33]

> Tragedy must try to evaluate all the known issues of life and attempt an estimate of that total validity, in this it is different and not complemental to comedy.[34]

> Great tragedy must spring from artists moral concern, the need to come to terms with the world, out of exploration of disaster find a vision of the relation of human joy to human suffering.[35]

> The end or scope of tragedy is to rectify or purge the passions... The plays of the Ancients are more correctly plotted, ours are more beautifully written; and if we can raise Passions as high on worse foundations, it shows our Genius in Tragedy is greater.[36]

> The major function of a tragedy is to produce some kind of beneficial effect upon the spectator through the execution of pity and fear.[37]

> The high and excellent Tragedy, that openeth the greatest wounds, and sheweth forth the Ulcers that are covered with tissue; that maketh Kinges feare to be Tyrants, and Tyrants manifest their tiranical humors; that, with sturring the affects of adhuration and commiseration, teacheth the uncertainty of this world, and upon how weake foundations golden roofes are builded.[38]

> Before we could not recognise tragedy as social crisis, now

---

[32] Catherine Belsey. The subject of Tragedy - Identity and Difference in Renaissance Drama.p.10

[33] Una Ellis-Fermor, The Jacobean Drama. p.4.

[34] Ibid. p.17

[35] Irving Ribner, Jacobean Tragedy - The quest For Moral Order. preface,p.xi

[36] John Dryden. Gilbert, Literary Criticism, The Works of John Dryden

[37] Earl R. Wasserman, The Pleasures of Tragedy

[38] Sir Philip Sidney. Raymond Williams, Modern Tragedy, p.24

commonly we cannot recognise social crisis as tragedy.[39]

It is clear then, that tragedy springs from social crisis, a need to explore the human condition, a moral concern, and that it must both explore and purge the passions and leave us with a beneficial effect. Tragedy, as the form of drama responsible for interpreting to man the conditions of his own being, is truly the genre of psychological drama. *Cracker*, in exploring not the who, but the why of crime is clearly placed within this form. Jacobean tragedy and film noir also most often explore not the who but the why and so have set the pattern which *Cracker* follows.

In order to make clear the comparisons I have made and the similarities I have found and proven, I have set out a table clearly indicating them. The divisions in the table (Fig. 1) then conform roughly to the sub-headings in part one and part two of this book. It will be clear on reading why certain elements have been grouped together and why certain elements cross over from one sub-heading to another.

I believe the evidence is so strong that many people recognised it instinctively as part of their cultural inheritance although perhaps not able or honest enough to acknowledge it as McGovern does. I have examined the historical, political and social factors existing during the late sixteenth and early seventeenth centuries, the pre and post world war II era and made comparisons to today in order to establish why different times could give rise to similar forms of drama. What emerges is the fact that unsettled times have all given rise to forms of tragedy with a psychological slant. Following investigation into historical contexts and conventions I have made a close comparison of *Cracker* to dramatic forms belonging to the Jacobean era and the genre of film noir. Many similarities emerged and I also established that Jacobean drama and film noir both draw strongly on their common history in Greek tragedy.

---

[39]  Raymond Williams, Modern Tragedy, p.63

FIG. 1

## POINTS OF CONTACT

| Jacobean Tragedy | Film Noir | Cracker |
| --- | --- | --- |
| period of political uncertainty post Elizabeth I | political uncertainty pre & post WW II | weak conservative government post Thatcher |
| alchemy (quasi- religious) New Science | Sci-fi, science saviour of mankind | cult religions, alternative medicine |
| period of depression following prosperity | 1930's depression / 1940's austerity | post 1980's slump |
| family relations out of joint | no family, adultery, | Fitz's family problems |
| Mother (sexually mature woman open to corruption) | femme fatale | Judith, Fitz's mother, Tina, etc. |
| good girl (virgin - Virtue, Chastity), sister or betrothed | girl friend, daughter of femme fatale, Bacall type | Fitz's daughter, Penhaligon (before temptation) |
| violence | yes | yes |
| writers in trouble with law (Crown) | writers censored & blacklisted | complaints to Broadcasting Standards Council |
| xenophobia - Spain & Italy | anti-communism, McCarthy witchhunts, | racism, strong immigration policy, race riots |
| sexual indulgence and perversion | yes | yes |
| self-punishment | yes | yes |

| Jacobean Tragedy | Film Noir | Cracker |
|---|---|---|
| disillusionment with the law | corrupt system and / or officers | officers obstruct truth, believe guilt without proof |
| love and / or misuse of position and power | corrupt system or system abused | abuse of authority |
| love of money | yes | yes |
| power of money to corrupt | yes | yes |
| hero against or outside the law | yes, often alone against corrupt system | tragic heroes against law, Fitz operates outside law |
| distrust of church (anti-papacy) | Catholic church linked to Mafia | church sex scandals |
| hero against or outside church | yes (church often = state) | Fitz lapsed Catholic, priests not above suspicion |
| parallel plots - secondary plot mimics or parodies underlines tragic theme | split plots - later connected | crime story (tragic) & private story (ironic) share theme |
| city (centre of rule) | city | city |
| false light torchlight | artificial light buildings, cars, neons | artificial light buildings, cars |
| shadows | chiaroscuro lighting | chiaroscuro lighting |
| night | night | night |

| Jacobean Tragedy | Film Noir | Cracker |
|---|---|---|
| disguise (Elizabethan / Jacobean definition includes mask, amnesia, drunkenness, duplicity) | yes | yes |
| intemperance | yes | yes |
| water - cleansing power of tears | water - waterfront, ritual washing, rain running down glass like tears | water cleansing sin, rain like tears |
| rain associated with storm obscuring light, symbol of evil | rain - obscuring light & truth - symbol of evil | rain - obscures light & truth, symbol of evil |
| hero avenging wrong, a revenger | yes | yes - many |
| hero seeking justice | yes | yes - Fitz, Bilborough |
| hero hoist by own petard | trapped by own mistake | tricked by own cleverness |
| disillusioned hero | yes | yes – both tragic & ironic |
| hero disappointed in love | yes | yes a/b |
| hero plays with fate | succumbs to fate, gambling, numbers racket | Fitz gambles |
| hero difficult to sympathise with and yet sympathetic | yes | yes |
| love of mother | implied | yes |
| loss or absence of father | father figure often dies | Fitz's father dead, other father figures die |

# PART 1 - HISTORICAL CONTEXTS & CONVENTIONS

"The drama of any period is an intricate set of practices of which some are incorporated - the known rhythms and movements of a residual but still active system - and some are exploratory - the different rhythms and movements of an emergent representation, rearrangement, new identification. Under real pressures these distinct kinds are often intricately and powerfully fused; it is rarely a simple case of the old drama and the new." [40]

I have already suggested that the time was right for the conception of a different type of detective series and that certain factors pointed the way to the creation of  a series with a psychological theme. In appendix two , Gub Neal explains the decision to mold *Cracker* as a psychological thriller. Both tragedy written in the Jacobean era and the film noirs of the 1940's and 1950's also have a psychological theme , and one must begin by asking what it was about all three times which could have given rise to similar forms of drama.

## UNSETTLED TIMES

The Elizabethan era was largely a time of stability in England, despite struggles against foreign powers and many attempts to overthrow or subvert the rule of Elizabeth I from inside and outside the country. Trade was good and mercantilism celebrated; it was possible to prosper by hard work or good fortune or both. One of the great fears of the Elizabethans was that order might give way to chaos, the danger stemming from the violation of the ordered hierarchy of nature, man and God. The new science, which drove the very sun from its course about the earth and permitted mutability about the moon, was seen as a force of chaos which disrupted the hierarchy. [41]  A number of writers of the period were known for their interest in science and occult lore. Chapman, Marlowe and Ralegh, along with astronomer Herriot, were members of the supposed 'School of Night' and suspected of atheism. [42] Elizabethan studies of melancholy connected the disorder with a sense that the times were out of joint. Fearfulness of melancholia was linked to the perception of rapid and undirected cultural

---

[40]   Raymond Williams On Television - Selected Writings. p.8.

[41]   A Study of Cyril Tourneur, Peter B. Murray. p.25.

[42]   Ibid. p.55.

change, sweeping away values and leaving behind powerless and alienated victims of destructive uncertainty. We have experienced a sweeping away of established values in the 1980's which has led to similar fears. Under the Thatcher government the old politics of class were broken up. Before Thatcherism there were clear sides, the state versus the market, and the unions versus the entrepreneurs. Before Thatcher, the Conservatives were the party of stability, the Labour party one of change; "she came from outside the party and reversed that."[43] Just as mercantilism was celebrated by the Elizabethans, the 'Sloanes' and the 'Yuppies'[44] of the 1980's found credit "became a fashion item".[45] Like the Jacobeans we are now suffering the consequences, and in the 1990's we are having to repay the overdraft.

Following Elizabethan order and unity came a period of instability and uncertainty, which began before Elizabeth's death in 1600 with dispute over who would follow her. James VI of Scotland was not crowned , as James I of England, until 1604 and was unpopular with many Englishmen even before he began to rule, not least for his religious affiliation. He proved to be even more unpopular than predicted.

## PATRONS

The theatre had prospered under Elizabeth I who was as good a patron as her father Henry VIII, even if a less enthusiastic performer. Masks were performed at the court of Henry VIII both as a pastime and on sanctioned occasions for the release and rehearnessing of social tension. With lavish costumes and display there was some affinity with Jacobean masque but Henry's court entertainments contained conflict, protest and mockery, and Elizabethan masks sometimes expressed criticism of the queen. As the century progressed, drama became a lively vehicle for political protest and experiment. Henry selected roles for himself, from hero to villain but never a god, dancing, jousting and paying for his fictions. Elizabeth, more decorous and parsimonious, footed the bill less often and had her most elaborate revels devised and put on by her nobles and lawyers of the Inns of Court.

---

[43] Martin Jacques (ed. The Independent), Peter York's Eighties, BBC2, 10.2.96.
[44] Terms coined by Peter York and Ann Barr. See the Sloane Ranger Handbook
[45] Anatole Kaletsky, Peter York's Eighties, BBC2, 10.2.96.

Herein lies one of the problems for the Jacobean theatre; he who pays the piper calls the tune. Though there were many theatre companies supported by patrons during James I reign, it was difficult to write demanding material for a monarch who fell asleep during performances and, on awaking, was likely to demand crossly that someone should dance. After the death of Elizabeth it seems to have become impossible to mythologise the English monarchy and even to believe an effective king was necessarily a good man. The changed temper of James I reign was surely responsible for this shift in attitude, for though subjects were aware of how hard-headed and devious Elizabeth was this knowledge co-existed with a view of her as phoenix, a secular Virgin Mary and magical icon of state. James had a very short honeymoon period. His foreign policy was pusillanimous, the Protestant cause betrayed at home and abroad, and he possessed ambiguous sexual tastes. A man who could think of nothing better to do with Ralegh than lock him up, James I was not charismatic let alone heroic, and his financial dodges, although cunning, were unworthy of a king.  As James' unpopularity grew, it also became impossible to write drama criticising him if one needed royal patronage, as most dramatists did. Nevertheless many companies survived even if their playwrights sometimes ended up in gaol. The names of the companies might give a clue as to patronage, for instance the Admiral's Men and the Earl of Worcestor's Men both run by Henlowe for whom Thomas Middleton wrote several pieces. Though not the most reputable companies they put on productions of *Dr. Faustus, The Shoemaker's Holiday* and *The White Devil.* Middleton also wrote for two children's companies, who performed in relatively small theatres, so-called private houses, and attracted a more cultivated and aristocratic audience than those at the Fortune and Rose theatres. They sponsored a group of young intellectual playwrights, mostly university men, of whom Middleton was one, with literary aspirations.

## DIVISION OF DRAMATIC FORM

During the Commonwealth most theatres were closed, considered unsuitable and dangerous by the Puritans, and by the Restoration, theatre had changed to the extent that the two patent theatres in London could hardly be filled. During the sixteenth and seventeenth centuries drama was the fictional mode which best addressed the audience. With drama performed at court and in the city, with an audience representative of social range and social mobility, drama before 1642 can be seen as a focus for contests of meaning and subjectivity. When theatre reopened in 1660, the stage became a place of affirmation of the common sense, the shared meanings of the new order. From this point on theatre developed in two directions for some considerable time, almost, one might say until today. What was acceptable as entertainment in Elizabethan and Jacobean theatre as a combination of drama, music and dancing separated into the 'serious theatre' patronised by the aristocracy and the 'popular theatre' or music hall of the common people. Catherine Belsey believes that liberal humanism locates drama above politics, as art, or below it, as entertainment. [46] Raymond Williams also draws attention to the division between 'legitimate' theatre and 'variety' theatre and agrees the division goes back to the Restoration. [47] It became, he says, a contrast of spectacle and pantomime with drama. In the eighteenth and nineteenth centuries the variety theatre developed intensively at several different social levels. Characteristic of urban development was the music hall, its very specific environment providing a mixture of singing, dancing, physical ability and comedy. There was an element of participation in music hall; drinking, the ability to move about, meet people and give a lively response to the performance which would have been familiar to audiences of Elizabethan and Jacobean theatre. Williams cites music hall as setting a precedent for an important part of television today. And it is, perhaps, only with the development of television this century possible for us to enjoy again an evening of mixed viewing, art and entertainment, without stigma or division.

---

[46] The Subject of Tragedy - Identity and Difference in Renaissance Drama. p.6-8
[47] Television, Technology & Cultural form. p.64

## THE DEPRESSION

In the meantime, the turn of the nineteenth century brought cinema to the people just in time to maintain spirits through another period of instability. Following the first World War, the twenties was a period of self-indulgence and celebration not unlike the Elizabethan era. The Wall Street crash in America and the Jarrow march in England were symbols of the Great Depression that swept the western world in the thirties, a time of financial instability , political unrest, high unemployment and social insecurity. Not surprising then that Freudian psychoanalysis was well under way in America before the forties began and informed a number of film genres, as well as surfacing in popular fiction, for example, Raymond Chandler's *The Little Sister.* Freud found a particular comfortable niche in 1940's thrillers with many crime films showing a personalisation of crime rather than making crime a social problem or a product of gangs. There was a fascination with the internal, subjectively generated criminal impulse which became widely recognised as a crucial characteristic of film noir. The incorporation of a psychoanalytic frame of reference served to explicate and contextualise a growing interest in the excesses provoked by psychical disturbance. The use of an elliptical and displaced mode of representation also proved useful in circumventing the Hayes code as the popularisation of psychoanalysis allowed audiences to decode underlying messages. There were transformations in the organisation of cinema in the forties in addition to extensive upheavals in the social and cultural environment. While there are films made before the forties which can be considered noir in genre, film noir emerged for certain when victory was in sight in 1944. The post-war era promised as much uncertainty as the war itself. There was the problem of women who had joined the workforce during the war having to readjust to life at home, the difficulties of men returning home to find no work, homes bombed, loved ones lost, in addition to the gargantuan task of rebuilding the economy. While war films looked at the renunciation of the individual and the glory of group achievement needed to keep hopes up, post war films tended towards a view that American society was a place to escape from rather than find one's place in. Peace also revived class divisions, another source of resentment. Sylvia Harvey says, "it may be argued that the ideology of national unity which was characteristic of the war period, and which tended to gloss over or conceal class divisions began to falter and decay, to lose its credibility once the war was over." [48] Urbanisation reached a peak in the 1940's. and almost at once, decline began. Stanley Aronowitz said, "The white working class was fated for dispersal; the centre of cities were reserved for the very poor and the relatively affluent."[49] The fear of a renewed depression lifted but left the cities desolate, the poor and the rich isolated in their separate worlds. The Hays Office tried to censor filmic depiction of the division in classes, calling for "less emphatic ... comparison of the poor in tenements ... and the rich in apartment houses." Joseph Breen wrote to Sam Goldwyn, regarding *Dead End*, "specifically, we recommend you do not show, at any time or at least that you do not emphasise, the presence of filth, or smelly garbage cans, or garbage floating in the river, into which the boys jump for a swim." [50]


## FAMILY RELATIONS

The idea that society had failed in its obligation to the individual was a theme common in films of the 1940's .Just as the romantic or 'screwball' comedies of the 1930's showed cultural change in the realm of love, marriage and sex, and sought to contextualise and disarm the recurring problems caused by the upheavals in heterosexual relations and the institution of marriage during the 1920's and early 1930's, now film noir would explore the insecurity felt by figures alienated by society. So we have a shift from romantic, dizzy heroines, who were convinced true happiness lay in marriage, to the discontented, passionate femme fatales in noir. Sylvia Harvey suggests that film noirs have negative representations of heterosexual relationships and the family as an institution because, in noir, the family is a metaphor for society; the family problems representing social discontent. From 1944, noir articulated scenarios of revolt against the family, for instance, adulterous relationships leading to the murder of the husband in *Double Indemnity* and *The Postman Always Rings Twice*, a couple living apart from, or pitted against the family or mainstream society in *They Live By Night* and *Gun Crazy* [51] The family is a constant state of upheaval in

---

[48] Women's Place and the Absent Family of Film Noir, Women In Film Noir (ed. Ann Kaplan).p.25

[49] False Promises, McGravithill, New York (1973) p.383

[50] Dark Cinema, p.137. (taken from Born To Lose - The Gangster Film in America, Eugene Roscow, Oxford University Press, New York (1978) p.281

[51] Ibid.

*Cracker*. Central is Fitz's own family; a wife who "in the first ten minutes leaves him, amazing,"[52] who wraps herself up in her job and then has an affair, a daughter who is taken away from him, a son he finds it difficult to relate to, even a Mother who he feels guilty about not visiting. All of this compounded by Fitz's affair with Penhaligon.

Later series continue the theme of family relations being 'out of joint', Judith can not cope with the new baby after it is born, Mark gets his girlfriend pregnant but she has a miscarriage. Similar family breakdowns were a common theme in Jacobean tragedy, as in classical tragedy before it, and also the subject of many Jacobean comedies. The breakdown of family is inherent in the crime story of *Cracker* as well. Kelly leaves the symbolic family of the monastery and immediately experiences problems; he is told he has a wife, but the woman turns out to be a liar. In the second *Cracker* story, Sean and Tina live apart from their families; Sean by implication has no-one, Tina is explicitly. 'at war' with her family. Some critics called it a '*Bonnie and Clyde*' relationship. although Wilson says, "it's only mentioned in the script, it's not really like that." [53] In the final story, Cassidy lives alone and, although he says he is thinking of getting married, his unmarried state is symbolic of his feared homosexuality. Noir "tough thrillers", as Frank Krutnik calls them, reveal an obsession with male figures who are internally divided and alienated from the culturally permissible or ideal parameters of masculine desire, identity and achievement. It is no longer permissible to kill for king and country and yet society demands that men behave as though the same codes are in force. This tension between external forces and internal drives is at the centre of film noir; sometimes the two forces are shown as facets of one character at others they are personified by two separate protagonists, one representing the individual the other society.

The noir theme of struggle of individual against society is not uncommon to Jacobean tragedy and also runs through *Cracker*; we return to Wilson "disenfranchised people" and McGovern's call for a right to be heard. Since both share common roots, it should not be difficult to see why. Jon Tuska wrote "Film noirs as a cultural perspective on life are in fact a movement towards negation the cultural origins of which can be traced all the way back

---

[52] Jimmy McGovern, authors interview, .2.96.
[53] Authors interview, 30.11.95.

to Greek and Roman tragedy." [54]  He suggests that noir tends to have a thematic relationship to the literary and a stylistic relationship to the cinematic and are about "not how but why a crime has been committed".[55] It would seem pertinent to see where the Greek connection begins.


## THE GREEKS - REVERSAL & RECOGNITION

Thirty two complete Greek dramas called tragedies survive, written by Aechylus, Sophocles, Euripedes and Seneca in addition to comedies written by Aristophanes.  Technically Seneca is not Greek, he was a Spaniard, educated in Rome who became Nero's tutor. In Aechylus and Sophocles, as opposed to Euripedes, gods introduce 'ate' into the soul via a 'daimon', in Latin 'daemon'. Aristotle distinguished between two kinds of tragedy; the Tragedy of Error, e.g. Oedipus Rex, and the Tragedy of Circumstances, e.g. Troades, for a tragedy of error is not necessarily to do with moral error although it might be. He says the best tragedy is composed to the law of cause and effect and not right and wrong. In terms of plot, tragedy is either simple or complex. In complex there is peripeteia and anagnorisis. The peripeteia is in effect a reversal, the tragic consequence of human effort producing exactly the opposite of the intention. In anagnorisis comes realisation of a truth, what was not known. Such recognition comes before or after the final catastrophe. As an example of this in *Cracker* one might choose as peripeteia the situation in *One Day A Lemming will Fly* when Fitz's efforts to find a murderer effect a confession from an innocent suspect, thus putting the unstoppable machine of justice into motion. The realisation of his error, the anagnorisis, comes too late to stop the final catastrophe. In Greek drama , if praxis, or progress, shows a woman gaining strength and power, then a man will be diminished. Such Greek heroines are Medea, Klytaimnestra, Antigone and Helen. A similar heroine from nineteenth century literature might be Nora, in Ibsen's *The Doll's House*, who gains the strength to leave Torrald as his world crashed irretrievably. This is a perfect model for the femme fatales of film noir.

---

[54]  Dark Cinema. introduction,p.xvi.

[55]  Ibid. p.xxii

## DEATH & DESIRE

In *Cracker* Fitz is weakened when Judith leaves him, he turns to drink for comfort. When she returns in a later episode, his drinking is less evident. Judith also behaves as a femme fatale by committing adultery with Graham and by her commitment to her job, which prevents her seeing Fitz. Tina is a prime example of a noir fatale, luring men for sex and then ending their lives completely. Ironically Sean who is strengthened when with Tina, some of her potence spilling over on to him, is weakened when separated from her. Once she is in prison, he begins to make fatal mistakes ending in his sacrifice of his own life as a demonstration of his love, yet again, the femme fatale at work. It is also possible to consider Penhaligon as a femme fatale, as she tempts Fitz away from his family. Though not fatal for Fitz, it is possibly this distraction which leads him to make the mistake about Cassidy, his mind being on other things.

The unrelenting power of fate and the dire effects of crime and wickedness is a theme found commonly in the work of Aechylus, whose primary focus is the justice of Providence. In his play *Eumenides* the Eumenides of the title are representations of equity and justice and are opposed by the Erinyes, or Furies, who represent revenge and retribution, whom they defeat at the end. Aechylus dressed the Furies in dark gowns and masks with snake hair, smeared with blood. In Greek myth the three Erinyes were born of the blood spilt on the earth when Uranus was castrated by his son Cronos. This makes sense of the division into order and chaos, being two halves of one whole, which carried through to the Elizabethans. The same blood which fell into the sea gave birth to Aphrodite, goddess of love, the act of castration giving both forces of pain and pleasure. This is the basis of the theme 'desire and death' which carries through to Jacobean tragedy and turns up in many film noirs. In *Agamemnon,* Klytaimnestra experiences sexual exhilaration at Kassandra's death. Kassandra is Agamemnon's mistress and is killed by Klytaimnestra's lover, Aigisthus. This is the same kind of excitement felt by Cora and Frank in the novel The *Postman always Rings Twice,* after they kill Cora's husband Nick. Cora's sexual arousal begins with her ripping her blouse to make it look as though she has been in the crashed car when it went over the cliff. "Rip me. Rip me" she cries. Frank hits her in the eye and then, "she was down there, and the breath was roaring in the back of my throat like I was some kind of animal, and my tongue was all swelled up in my mouth and blood pounding in it ... I had her."[56]

Tuska describes the sex Cora and Frank have after the murder as "harking back to the sexual exhilaration of Klytaimnestra."[57] The same feeling of sexual excitement is felt by Sean and Tina in *To Say I Love You* after they kill Cormack in the alley. Tina lures Cormack into the alley with a promise of 'payment in kind', "he thrusts her against a wall, kisses her roughly. His hands are everywhere." Sean watches, concealed,

> "He's rigid with fury and disgust. At last he moves, approaches Cormack, brings half a brick crashing down on the back of his head, Cormack falls. Sean goes down with him, hammering away with the brick. Hammering away...   They start to run....She crashes into a dustbin, stumbles. He stoops to pick her up. Their eyes meet. He pins her against the wall. They've never felt so sexually aroused, so voracious. They begin to make rough, torrid love..."[58]

Although Andy Wilson admits there are similarities between his film and *The Postman Always Rings Twice* his idea for the scene did not "come from any particular movie. It's a theme from the ether... It's a thematic thing in literature as a whole. You can point to any one of a hundred different examples . In Jacobean tragedy its easy because they actually personify the archetype as a rigid structural item.... It's a truth that violence creates a feeling of power. If you feel you're a disenfranchised person and you don't have any hope, an act of random violence will often make you feel better for a few hours, like drugs. It's exactly the same as a person who goes out on a Friday night looking for a fight in a pub. If they win they feel great, if they lose they feel crap, but that doesn't stop them going out every Friday night like a drug." [59] While Wilson cites the addictive qualities of violence and their link to a feeling of power, McGovern is more specific in linking death and desire. In *Cracker* he has Fitz compare Sean and Tina's feelings to rapture which met the heroes returning from war.

---

[56] The Postman always rings Twice, James M. Cain. This sex scene is in the novel, but was cut from the film. In the film Frank and Cora have already consummated their love by symbolically plunging into the sea as waves crash onto a moonlight beach.
[57] Dark Cinema, p.93
[58] To Say I Love You. Final script, sc.43.p.77-78
[59] Authors interview, 30.11.95.

FITZ : "Remember the soldiers coming home from the Falklands War ?... All those women lining the quayside, waving their knickers and bras. Patriotism ? No. <u>Lust.</u> Those men had killed and those women <u>wanted</u> them. What's death, Panhandle ?"
PENHALIGON : "The finest aphrodisiac in the world', Doctor Fitzgerald." [60]


## SACRIFICE

Sophocles, the foremost dramatist of the Periclean age, had a profound sense of religious reverence, he was a priest in the cult of Alcon. Whilst he believed the guilty would suffer, he was aware that innocence is often unprotected and the guiltless seem to suffer undeservedly, another theme found in McGovern's work today. The great challenge for Sophocles's heroes is not simply to endure suffering brought about by reversal of fortune but to respond with greatness of soul. It might be said that Fitz endures the suffering in his personal life with greatness of soul, other characters in *Cracker* certainly do. Kelly, the suspect in *The Mad Woman In The Attic* responds to aggressive interrogation with deep insight and generosity telling Fitz, "There's a great sadness in your life, [61] giving the first indication of his innocence.

Euripedes' central theme in his plays was the idea of love as the 'primum mobile' of all creation. This prompted ridicule of him by Aristophanes. The Jacobeans were fond of the idea of love as a creative and destructive force and the concept of true love being eternal. One of the paradoxes of eternal love its tragic consequences are also intensified. In *The Second Maiden's Tragedy* written in 1611, the Lady kills herself in order to perpetuate love beyond the grave,

"His lust may part me from thee, but death, never;
Thou canst not lose me there, for, dying thine,
Thou dost enjoy me still. Kings cannot rob thee." [62]

This act of supreme sacrifice is like the one made by Sean for Tina at the end of *To Say I Love You*. Sean would rather die to show his love for Tina than have the "one lousy hour" with her that Fitz promises. As McGovern

---

[60]  To Say I Love You. Final script. sc.50. p.90-91
[61]  Final script. sc. 57. p. 88
[62]  Thomas Middleton. Act III, iii. 144-6

says, "it would never be enough. For most men one hour is not enough but for him its nothing. Particularly with a crippling speech impediment like that. Its a dramatic gesture."

## VIOLENCE & CENSORSHIP

Euripedes was also friendly with philosophers, a dangerous thing at a time when there was no freedom of thought in Athens. In 432BC freethinkers were subjected to public enquiry into the possible effects of their ideas on 'right thinking' Athenians. Anaxagoras was fined and banished, Diagoras fled, so did Protagoras. Socrates was put to death, and Euripedes may have been indicted. Jon Tuska compares this censorship of ideas to the situation that arose in Germany in 1930's and America in the 1940's [63] Film noir was used by directors to make covert political statements at a time when speaking out could be dangerous. For example, Abraham Polonsky , himself blacklisted later on, equated organised crime with big business and the law and got away with it in *Force of Evil.* [64]

There are similarities to the way the Elizabethans distrusted the 'new science' for its ability to disrupt the established order, and they were no strangers to censorship. Despotic regimes have always recognised, though in rather different terms, the close relationships between fiction and politics, and have subjected works of art to detailed censorship. Tudor monarchs took drama under increasing central control from the mid sixteenth century on. There was an elaborate system of licensing plays and players which indicates the level of government concern with the political implications of drama. The Stuarts extended royal control by converting the prominent London companies into servants of members of the Royal Family , and the jurisdiction of the Revels Office increased. By the seventeenth century the Master of Revels was responsible for ensuring no seditious material was presented on stage. He was empowered to require alteration of single words, passages or whole scenes, or suppress the play entirely. Texts were often changed and playwrights imprisoned.

---

[63]   Dark Cinema, American Film Noir in Cultural Perspective. p.22
[64]   Force of Evil, Enterprise, (1948). Based on the novel Tucker's People.

This kind of censorship continues today with the "moral hoodlums" [65] criticism of *Cracker.* The Broadcasting Standards Council , the modern day equivalent of the Revels Office perhaps, upheld complaints about scenes in *The Mad Woman In The Attic* and *To Say I Love You.* Granada "says sorry to viewers" after the Council found scenes of sex and murder in the alley in "To Say I Love You" "unnecessarily violent" and ruled that this was "profoundly shocking" and "went beyond acceptable limits". They also found that viewers were right to be offended by mortuary scenes that were "too graphic" and the blood-stained body in the railway carriage in "The Mad Woman In The Attic". One shot of the dead girl's body being zipped into a body bag is very reminiscent of the same treatment given to Laura Palmer's body in Twin Peaks. [66] However the Council did not uphold complaints about offensive language, including the phrase "buggering the Pope." Granada acknowledged the "strong images and language" but explained they were thought necessary to portray the criminal mind. [67] As Catherine Belsey says, "A specific discourse is always embattled, forever defending the limits of what is admissible, legitimate or intelligible. [68]

Some shots were removed by Granada from *The Mad Woman In The Attic* as a result when it was re-edited for release in a movie version, but no further editing was done on the alley scenes. Andy Wilson told me he had already removed one sound effect, of the sound of the brick hitting Cormack's head, at the request of "the powers that be" at the Network Centre, who operate a form of Revels Office type censorship internally within ITV, but was not subject to further censorship when he re-edited his story. He says, "Sally (Head) said 'you're really lucky, they had to say something, so they said something, but they're letting you go lightly', I just took the music up a bit higher and brought that sound effect down." Justifying the scene he says, "You think, how can I make this scene appear to be true, what's the motivational factor that will make these actors able to do it with a truth and a depth that will make it not pornographic. I'm a person who's very moral, I won't do anything gratuitous." He was not surprised by the criticism but finds it worrying that while in his scene "You don't see a thing, just a trickle of blood down the guy's forehead," in programmes

---

[65] Andy Wilson, authors interview, 30.11.95.

[66] Twin Peaks, David Lynch, dir., BBC2, 1990-91.

[67] Daily Post, 18.12.93. Glasgow Daily Record, 18.12.93. Daily Mirror, 18.12.93.

[68] The Subject of Tragedy - Identity and Difference in Renaissance Drama. p.6

Bilborough's (& audience) POV of the body

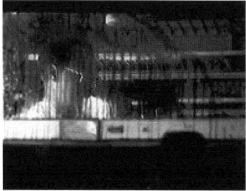

The dead girl's blood running down the mirror like rain down a window.

Flashback - Kelly's POV of the body

"...something for the album ?"

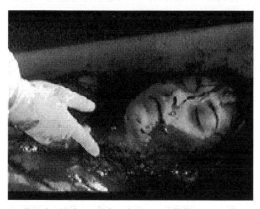

Pathologist points to the fatal wound

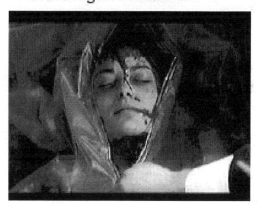

Jacqui is zipped into a body bag - reminiscent of Laura Palmer in Twin Peaks.

The Broadcasting Standards Council upheld viewers complaints about gory shots of the body at the post mortem.

watched by his young daughter, "like that mountie thing, *Due South*, you see bullets exploding in people's bodies every week, and *Power Rangers* represents even more scenes of violence." [69]

It is interesting to find that realistic scenes of violence are held as being "beyond acceptable limits" while less realistic portrayals of violence go unquestioned. Interesting too, that sex and violence are still considered shocking but language calling into question the church passes criticism. A sign that, yet again, the power of the church is either diminishing or being called into question itself.

Seneca, who created the formal divisions in drama which triumphed as the five-act play throughout Renaissance Europe, was no stranger to violence. He wrote ten tragedies which can not be divorced from his philosophy which was basically that a man must bring his life into accord with the laws of nature and in this way conform to divine will. Foremost in living is to value least what can be taken away and resigned to what Fortune may bring. He had a penchant for violent horror. It was convention in the Greek theatre for violent acts to be committed 'off', but Seneca has Medea kill both her boys on stage in his *Medea*. Elizabethan plays were less squeamish. Seneca's Oedipus has justification for blinding himself, less offensive than the blinding in Shakespear's *King Lear*. In *Titus Andronicus* Shakespear's hero cuts his own hand off and Lavinia is also mutilated. In *The Spanish Tragedy,* written by Kyd, Hieronimo, bites off his own tongue.


## DIALOGUE

Seneca also used dialogue in a similar way to the 'hard-boiled' writers of 1940's noir. In short dialogue sequences he used sichomythia, a technique of line by line interchange between characters. Examples of this type of interchange can be found in Jacobean tragedy, particularly when there is some tension between protagonists, for example in *The Changeling:,* when Alsemero challenges his wife with the fact of her adultery:

> BEATRICE: "Is there cause ?"
> ALSEMERO : "Worse; your lust's devil, Your adultery !"

---

[69]  Authors interview, 30.11.95.

BEATRICE : "Would any but yourself say that, 'Twould turn him to a villain."
ALSEMERO : "It was witnessed By the counsel of your bosom, Diaphanta."
BEATRICE : "Is your witness dead then ?"
ALSEMERO : "'Tis to be feared It was the wages of her knowledge. Poor    soul, She lived not long after the discovery."[70]

This dialogue technique will be familiar to readers of Cain, Hamnett and Chandler as well as viewers of film noir. Some critics, mentioned earlier, also compared McGovern's writing style to Chandler. The similarity is particularly noticeable in dialogue exchanges between Fitz and women, often with filmic references. For example take this exchange between Fitz and his wife Judith.

> EXT. STREET - EVENING, ROCK AND ROLL PLAYING. PAN ACROSS CINEMA BOARD ' MADE IN AMERICA' - ODEON FIRST CHOICE. FITZ AND JUDITH WALK ALONG STREET.
> JUDITH: "Bogart at the end of Casablanca
> FITZ: He doesn't die."
> JUDITH: His motive's still pure."
> FITZ : Pure-ish. Jimmy Cagney at the end of 'Angels With Dirty Faces'."
> JUDITH: "No".
> FITZ: Come on - Pat O'Brien asks him to scream - he says, 'don't do this to me, don't...'" [71]

Another example is a scene between Fitz and Tina after she has been arrested.

> PENHALIGON LOOKS FROM FITZ TO TINA.
> TINA: "Get rid of her"
> FITZ: "Panhandle ?"
> TINA: "Get rid of her."
> FITZ : "You don't like her ?"
> TINA : "Get rid of her."
> FITZ: "Why don't you like her ?"
> TINA : "Can I have one ?" (A CIGGY) [72]

---

[70]    Act V, Sc. III.
[71]    One Day A Lemming Will Fly, sc.1.dialogue differs from script which continues "... scream. 'You can't ask me to do that , Father. You're taking away the only thing I have left.'."
[72]    To Say I Love You, sc.131.p.270.

This type of 'banter' is typical of Fitz's character, whoever he is talking to. Fitz is also prone to frequent off the cuff wisecracks, a well known feature for defusing uncomfortable situations; we most often joke about what frightens us most. In film noir, under the jurisdiction of American cultural and moral values, the wisecrack is seen as a sign of independence. Combined with a refusal to accept the rules of propriety and contempt for politeness when it serves as a tie, it is seen as a mark of experience.


## THE FIVE ACT STRUCTURE

Shakespeare inherited the five-act structure from Seneca, and refined it with precision. The acts are: situation, conflict, crisis, reversal and catastrophe. In his finest tragedies, for instance, *Macbeth*, recognition comes with catastrophe. In Shakespeare these five parts do not correspond directly to the five acts, but are always present as divisions of narrative and dramatic structure. Tuska says this can be seen in the narrative construction of film noir from *Double Indemnity* made in 1944 to *Body Heat* made in 1981.[73] *Double Indemnity* has a classic five-act structure. The Situation; is expressed employing flashback, as Neff confesses we see his wound is fatal. The Conflict: Phyllis wants Neff to help her murder her husband, Neff resists before giving in. Neff is attracted to Phyllis and the money they will obtain, but it is his boredom with his job which is the clinching factor, he hopes to beat the system. The Crisis: there are frustrations and mishaps over the killing of Dietrichson and the attempt to make it look like an accident. The Reversal: Neff realises Phyllis has no feeling for him, she is promiscuous with her daughter's boyfriend and intends to murder Neff. He finds out about her previous murders. Neff and Phyllis shoot each other, Phyllis dies. The Recognition: Keyes finds Neff dictating his confession in his office. Keys lights Neff's cigarette, before Neff had always lit Keyes cigar as he had no match, a symbol of impotence. Neff tells Keys, "I love you too", an ironic remark made in half jest. Neff realises he has made all the wrong choices. Biller Wilder called this scene, "the love of a father for his surrogate son" and "faded out on those two faces" rather than use the planned execution scene whose set had cost $150,000 to build.[74] *Cracker* demonstrates a five-act structure, take for example, *One Day A Lemming*

---

[73] Dark Cinema, p.39-41

[74] Maurice Zolotow, Biller Wilder in Hollywood. Putnam's, New York (1977) p.119

*Will Fly.* The Situation: A body is found hanging in the wood, a boy is missing from home. The Conflict: If the couple report the body their adultery will become known. Cassidy is arrested under circumstantial evidence. The Conflict: The police need a suspect. Cassidy denies the murder then confesses. The Reversal: Cassidy retracts his confession to Fitz but will not tell the police. The Recognition: Fitz realises he is responsible for the arrest of an innocent man, the killer is still at large.


## LITERARY ROOTS

While the Greek tragedies led directly to tragic dramas of the Elizabethan and Jacobean eras, film noir had roots in a literary tradition as well. Gothic fiction is a precursor of detective fiction from which most film noir springs. It began with Horace Walpole's *Castle of Otranto* (1791), followed by Ann Radcliffe's *The Mysteries of Udolpho* (1794) and *The Italian* (1797). In 1796, *The Monk* was written by Matthew Gregory Lewis, followed by Mary Shelley's *Frankenstein* in 1818. In the nineteenth century, Hawthorne, Melville and Poe continued the gothic theme, Poe creating the detective story. Henry Levin wrote of Poe that he, "prefers to dwell on the psychology of crime rather than upon the ethics of guilt." [75] What Poe created became the classic detective story, the gothic and romantic elements were rejected but surfaced again in the 'hard-boiled' detective story of the "Black Mask" school, combined with a milieu that produced a corpse.

The *Black Mask* magazine was published by 'Capt." Joseph T. Shaw[76] , and although it was considered 'pulp' fiction it encouraged many writers of note. Shaw published Hamnett and persuaded him to move from short stories to novels. Raymond Chandler also wrote for *Black Mask*, quitting when Shaw left and submitting to *Dime Detective* magazine. Many Chandler novels began as short 'pulp' stories. *Farewell My Lovely*, the second Philip Marlowe novel, combines parts of plots from stories like *The Man Who Liked Dogs, Try The Girl* and *The Blonde* . The tradition of pulp fiction stemmed from the dime novels of the 1910's and at first came from the English style classical detective. There were many adaptations of 'hard-boiled' novels and short

---

[75] The Power of Blackness, 1958

[76] The Black Mask school is dealt with in depth by Jon Tuska in Dark Cinema, chap. 2 The Hostages of Fate.

stories; David Bordwell estimates that almost twenty per cent of film noirs between 1941 and 1948 were adaptations, which does not include imitations or reworks of 'hard-boiled' sources by writers who moved to Hollywood [77] In the 1930's there were no films to match the intensity of the 'hard-boiled' novels. Novels by Hamnett, Cain and Chandler[78] published by the respectable but adventurous publisher A.A. Knopf in New York often had content thought unsuitable under the Hays code. William Leuchtenburg says the Hays Office, "added hypocrisy to sex by insisting on false moralisations and the 'moral ' ending."[79] MGM bought the film rights to *The Postman Always Rings Twice* in 1934 and *Double Indemnity* was purchased by Paramount in 1936, but they had to wait twelve and eight years respectively to be made. 'Hard-boiled' novels were known for their economical dialogue and were terse and quick to read. James M. Cain wrote both the novels mentioned, *Double Indemnity* based on the notorious Snyder Gray case of 1927, and both are hard hitting. However it was Chandler's script, co-written with director Billy Wilder, which gave the 1944 film *Double Indemnity* much of its sinister style. Later remakes of *Double Indemnity* and *The Postman Always Rings Twice* are lifeless in comparison to these noir classics. Tuska describes Chandler writing in a style which "imparted overtones, echoes and images, in which images dominated even obscured the linear narrative." [80]  Chandler had criticised Hammett for not doing this, although he praised Hammett for taking "murder out of the Venetian vase and dropping it in the alley" and for his "rather revolutionary debunking of both language and material of fiction." [81] Hammett strove for clarity, simplicity and action, Chandler, with his English public school education, was more classical. He wrote to his publisher Hamish Hamilton, "I am not only literate but intellectual, much as I dislike the term. It would seem that a classical education might be a rather poor basis for writing novels in a hard-boiled vernacular. I happen to think otherwise. A classical education saves you being fooled by pretentiousness, which is what most fiction is full of." [82]  Perhaps this gives a further clue to *Cracker's* success, since many of its instigators enjoyed a classical education, allowing them to give structure to stories inspired by experience of life. His classical

---

[77]  Frank Krutnik, In A Lonely Street, p.33

[78]  Chandler also published with Hamish Hamilton

[79]  The Perils of Prosperity: 1914 - 1932, Harper & Row, New York (1962) p.282

[80]  Dark Cinema, p.73

[81]  Frank Krutnik, In A Lonely Street, p.40.

[82]  Frank McShane, The Life of Raymond Chandler (Dutton) New York, 1796.p.10

education did not prevent Chandler writing about the seedy side of life. Frederic Jameson describes him as "the least politically correct writer of all our modern writers, Chandler faithfully gives vent to everything racist, sexist, homophobic, and otherwise socially resentful and reactionary in the American collective consciousness, enhancing these unlovely feelings - which are however almost exclusively nobilised for striking and essentially visual purposes, that is to say, for aesthetic rather than political ones - by a homoerotic and male-bonding sentimentalism that is aroused by honest cops and gangsters with hearts of gold, but finds its most open expression in the plot of *The Long Goodbye*."[83] (sic.) One might almost be describing McGovern.

## EXPRESSIONISM

While the fiction of film noir came from the 'hard-boiled' novel, its style came largely from German expressionism [84] Hollywood had always attracted émigrés and the flight from Hitler started in 1933  Expressionism was not new in America of the 1940's, it was at work there and in Russia from at least 1915, and perhaps even earlier in France and Denmark, but the new influx of German technicians revived its influence. Billy Wilder, the director of *Double Indemnity* was one of these, having worked as a writer in Vienna and Berlin before going to America. Fritz Lang and Robert Siodmak were among many others who also fled the Hitler regime. [85]  As Vernet says,  noir "assures the triumph of European artists even as it presents American actors." [86]  Actors were more natural, less glamorous; Lauren Bacall rather than Margaret Lindsay, and Bogart, who had a very American look. Much is owed to Bogart, who was so unlike the 'English' mastermind detectives like Basil Rathbone or William Powell, and starred in film noirs such as *In A Lonely Place*. [87]  The war economy meant less exteriors, or less real exteriors, and restricted studio space. Expressionist techniques made the

---

[83]  Shades of Noir - The Synoptic Chandler, p.37

[84]  Marc Vernet, Film Noir On The Edge Of Doom, Shades of Noir, p.7.

[85]  Director Robert Siodmak went on to make film noirs in America, many starting as 'B' pictures. He was brother to Kurt, screenwriter and science-fiction novelist. This link could suggest how Andy Wilson, with his early interest in science-fiction, came to make the most noir-like "Cracker".

[86]  Ibid. p.1

[87]  In A Lonely Place, Santana, 1950. Bogart starred as gifted, but volatile, Hollywood screenwriter, Dixon Steele.

41

most what was available with careful use of constricted space contributing to the claustrophobic feel of many film noirs. Black and white, contrast, opposition, light, shadows and oblique lines as part of composition were all important in expressionism and I shall consider some of these in more depth in relation to *Cracker* later.

## PREJUDICIAL BELIEFS

In setting the background of time, situation and genres which have influenced the production of *Cracker*, it only remains to add the dimension of the effects of xenophobia, homophobia and religion. It may seem strange to group these items together, but they are inextricably linked. McGovern's writing is informed by his Catholicism to a very large extent, and although "its not just the Pope who makes you guilty,"[88] his writing bears many religious scars. Like many lapsed Catholics, myself included, McGovern has a love-hate relationship with religion. For instance he writes, "I grew up during the reign of Pope Pius 12th. He was fiercely opposed (like this Polish misogynist we've got now ) to birth control and people reckon it was his influence that led to the birth of so many babies." [89] But McGovern admits that, "every time I've needed priests, they've been there. And they've been good priests, not the priest who taught me, not those Jesuits, but ordinary priests. When I came away from that school I didn't want to know anything about the Catholic faith or the priesthood or priests, but I got to be in my thirties and changed slightly. Remember the Church in the aftermath of Hillsborough in 1989, the Catholic Church was wonderful in our city. And on the death of my father there was a wonderful Catholic priest. At times of grief they've been there and at times of joy. I've had my kids christened Catholic. One or two individual priests that's the best advert for the faith."[90]

 He is at once fascinated by religion and the church and repelled by the hypocrisy within it, notice the difference between the admiration for individual priests and his rather hostile attitude to the 'establishment' of the

---

[88] Simon Cellan Jones, authors interview, 30.11.95.

[89] Letter to author, 1994. McGovern continues, "Bollocks. It was Clark Gable. Clark's eyes would twinkle; and the next minute it's moonlight on the beach and orgasmic waves crashing in. Clark never fumbled for a jonnie or got his underpants caught round his ankles so woe betide any man who did. I'm serious. Honest."

[90] Desert Island Discs, TX: 14.1.96.

church. McGovern has explored the problems caused by the Church's attitude to sex, for parishioners and priests, in *Cracker* and *Priest*. Homosexual relationships, priests with lovers, wives who kill to preserve the sanctity of marriage, the loss of faith, have all been explored. In *Cracker* it is the role of the confession, learnt by Catholics at an early age, which moves so easily into the detective series. It is important to remember that McGovern made Fitz a lapsed Catholic like himself, and this loss of faith becomes a symbol of Fitz's lack of faith in himself, not a reason for his drinking and gambling, but a symbol of the void in himself which causes his addictions. Once the ritual of confession has begun in *The Mad Woman In The Attic,* both men betray their shared religion and their backgrounds.

> FITZ: "A number. Any number."
> KELLY: "Two, double one, nine, O, two."     (his mothers co-op number)
> FITZ: "Alpha, beta, gamma, delta....."
> KELLY: "Epsilon, seta, eta, theta..."  (Greek numbers - sign of a grammar school education)
> FITZ: "Who made you ?"
> KELLY : "God made me."
> FITZ: "Why did God make you ?"
> KELLY: "God made me to know Him, love him and serve Him in this world, and to be happy with Him forever in the next."   (Catholic catechism)
> FITZ: "A writer."
> KELLY: "Dickens."     (education again)[91]

Fitz will also often come out with words or phrases which betray his religion, for example, "They'll crucify you for it... They'll crucify you out of fear."[92]

It is fear, fear of the unknown which leads to xenophobia and homophobia which is partly why I link them to religion. In *One Day A Lemming Will Fly* it is the public and police attitude to the threat of homosexuality which provokes a lynching mob into action against Cassidy, becoming almost more important than whether or not he is a murderer. Cassidy betrays his own homosexual feelings towards Tim, the dead boy, when he reveals to Fitz, "I hardly knew him at all. Bit of a loner. Bit effeminate, gets picked on." The scene takes place in the school gym, Cassidy alternating between 'hammering' and 'embracing' a punchbag. Cassidy fells the need to assert his normality, "I'm thinking of getting married," he tells Fitz and Penhaligon,

---

[91]  Sc. 67. p. 104-105
[92]  The Mad Woman In The Attic, sc. 57. p.91.

1. Cassidy hammering the punchbag.

2. The punchbag is used in this 3-shot to balance the composition, but also isolates Cassidy from Fitz & Penhaligon

3 & 4. Cassidy embraces the punchbag then hammers it again, signifying his problematic relationship with Tim - the punchbag becomes Tim.

5. Fitz at home.

6. Judith refuses to drink with Fitz.

5,6 & 7. Fitz turns to the bottle again to try to resolve his problems at home and at work.

6. Fitz with Beck & Cassidy at the hotel.

but other words reveal more, "just keeping your hands off the little bastards."
[93] Cassidy reveals his fears about his own homosexual tendencies.
Evidence of Beck's homophobia also turns up in *One Day A Lemming Will Fly*, after the arrest of Cassidy for Tim's murder. After Beck taunts Cassidy and calls him a "sick bastard", Fitz psychoanalyses Beck while he tries to intimidate Cassidy further.

> FITZ: "The boys ignored you , didn't they. Beck ?....One boy in particular. You wanted to be near him, you wanted to hold him. It bothered you.....You thought you were gay..."[94]

Later Beck shaves off his moustache because Cassidy's girlfriend Lesley has suggested it is a sign of homosexuality. McGovern says that Lorcan Cranitch, the actor who played Beck, collaborated on his character, offering several ideas towards his background and motivation. It was Cranitch who suggested that Beck had come over from Ireland when he was about fourteen, a fact mentioned in the above scene. Cranitch also felt that Beck had a problem in relating sexually because he had been "taken under the wing" of older girls when he arrived as an innocent and, they agreed, had suffered a sexual identity crisis. He is still unsure of his masculinity and needs to prove it to himself and the world. Later in *Cracker*, after Penhaligon's rape, it will emerge that Beck idolised the policeman who walked the beat outside his house, perhaps as a replacement for his real father who was absent or brutal, and had a strong love for his mother.


## SIN

*One Day A Lemming Will Fly* revolves around the Catholic concept of Sin. Once you understand the idea of Sin; Original, Actual, Mortal and Venial, it is easy to find the reason why Cassidy is so willing to go along with the police and admit his guilt. I will give definitions of Sin in order to illustrate my point.

> "ORIGINAL SIN - Through the sin of Adam we were all conceived in original sin. This sin is the guilt of Adam passed on to us .It is called original sin because we contract it in our very origin. ACTUAL SIN is the sin we ourselves commit. It is any word, thought, deed or

---

[93] Sc. 31.p.34-35
[94] Sc.99. p.163-168

omission against the law of God. That is, it is any breaking of God's commandments - either of those which He gave to Moses on Mount Sinai, or those which He has given us by Christ and His Church. Or, lastly, it is the doing of anything which our conscience tells us to be wrong. An actual sin is mortal or venial. MORTAL SIN, that is, deadly or killing sin, is that which offends God grievously. It is a sin that does great injury to the honour of God, or to our neighbour or to ourselves. Idolatry, murder, impurity and the like are mortal sins. Such sins deprive the soul of sanctifying grace, which is the supernatural life of the soul. VENIAL SIN is a less grievous offence against God. For instance, slight passions, little lies of excuse, wilful distractions in prayer and the like. They are called venial, or pardonable, sins because they are more easily forgiven than mortal sins. Yet next to mortal sin, venial sin is the greatest evil in the world." [95] Listed after these definitions are "THE PUNISHMENTS DUE TO SIN. The due punishment of original sin is the loss of heaven and the deprivation of the sight of God for ever. For actual sin we deserve to be punished with pain and torment after death. For mortal sin we deserve to be punished for ever in the fire of hell. For venial sin we deserve to be punished with some temporal punishment, or punishment that will last for a time, in the fire of purgatory."[96]

No wonder, then, that Catholics invented the ritual of the confessional. Director Cellan Jones agreed that Cassidy had been guilty "in thought" and believed he ought to be punished because of the homosexual feelings he had harboured for Tim. We also agreed that Cassidy probably felt guilty as he believed he could have saved the boy from suicide if he had not been so homophobic. He was, therefore, guilty of murder because of his 'sin of omission'. In *The Mad Woman In The Attic* Kelly is also willing to confess when he starts to believe that he may have committed the murder. In the hospital he tells Dr. Turner,

> "My being like this is annoying you, I know. But it's <u>destroying</u> me. Prove to me I did this and, I promise, I'll confess, I'll sign anything you want." [97]

In Jacobean plays Sin is often depicted as blind, suggesting that the sinner gropes in a dark world until he stumbles on the path that leads to inevitable disaster. For instance; Follywit pursues his grandfather's mistress, [98]

---

[95] Rev. A. Bromley Crane, Facts of Faith.Burns & Oates, London (1885) p.16-17
[96] Ibid. p.17
[97] Sc.45. p.57
[98] A Mad World My Masters, Middleton, 1604-6

Lussurio turns to his worst enemy for help,[99] Beatrice makes an accomplice of the man she loathes.[100] There is a sense of human baseness, a sense of justice which prevails, a mysterious moral force which closes their eyes, misdirects their steps and leads them to prepare their own retribution. One discovers that Sin is a form of stupidity. Many Jacobean plays portrayed and condemned Sins such as adultery, incest, rape, murder and well as the venial Sins of covetousness, greed and avarice. Sex is often linked with overindulgence in both eating and drinking, so Spurio declares " I was begot / After some gluttonous dinner - some stirring dish / Was my first father" [101] and Vindici says, " Oh Dutch lust ! Fulsome lust ! / Drunken procreation, which begets so many drunkards;" [102] The only Sin to compare with this for power to corrupt is money, often in the form of gold. Bacon said, "Great riches have sold more men than they have bought." [103] In Jacobean times a subtle word play is allowed by the use of 'angels' both as gold coin and instruments of God, so Vindici can declare, "forty angels can make four score devils."[104] Gold and women, that is the temptation offered by their presence , are inextricably linked in *The Revenger's Tragedy* as dual evils of the world. Vindici says, "Were't not for gold and women there would be no damnation." [105] A theme contemporary to today.

The combination of religion, fear, guilt and confession runs through much of McGovern's work, which is not surprisingly why he writes such good psychological detective stories. McGovern is able to voice through his characters and situations many of the fears felt in contemporary society, just as Jacobean playwrights and creators of film noirs did in their time. The rampant xenophobia which spread through America in the 1940's and 1950's was focused by McCarthyism. Just as soon as the old enemy in Germany has been defeated, America began the Cold War against the threat of Communism from Russia. With the threat more imagined than real, the McCarthy 'witch hunts' nevertheless sought out and punished their enemies with hysterical zeal. Many Hollywood writers and directors, with their European backgrounds, suffered and were blacklisted, some for many

---

[99] The Revenger's Tragedy, Tourneur (?) , 1607

[100] The Changeling, Middleton & Rowley, 1622

[101] The Revenger's Tragedy, (I.ii. 178-180)

[102] Ibid. (I.iii. 59-60)

[103] Peter York's Eighties, BBC2, TX. 10.2.96.

[104] The Revenger's Tragedy, (II.i.88)

[105] Ibid. (I.i. 253)

years. Marc Vernet suggests that the French viewed America as an "imperialist menace" which threatened to impose values and culture that were "non-French". He goes on to say that noir was seen as "signs of the unhealthy character of capitalism" and because of this the films were given a high value in France for their critique of the American system. By affirming this and emphasising the importance of European technicians and drawing attention to Hammett's membership of the Communist party French film critics gave themselves a means to justify a lore that was forbidden.[106] What is clear, then, is the acceptance of the fact that film noirs were a means to criticise the system whilst remaining in it. A later development of dealing with the fear of 'Reds under the bed' and invasion by communist forces was the translation of communists into aliens, thus the popularity of invasion from outer space in so many 1950's science fiction films. Again it is the fear of the unknown, a fear of even discussing the problem, which leads to writers transposing situations to a venue where the issues can be aired.

## THE ITALIAN CONNECTION

The Jacobeans had a similar method of dealing with religious and political problems at a time when punishment was likely to be more severe than a prison sentence. Italy was often used as a setting by Jacobean playwrights as a convenient model to represent English evils, whether native or imported. It was thought in Elizabethan society that Italy was a place where the English upper class could learn to exploit the poor and from where many nobles had brought vices to England. A popular rhyme of the time was,

"An Englishman Italianate, Is a devil incarnate" [107]

Nashe calls Italy,

" the Acadamie of man-slaughter, the sporting place of murther, the Apothocary-shop of poyson for all Nations: how many kind of weapons hast thou invented for malice ?" [108]

---

[106] Marc Vernet, Film Noir On The Edge of Doom (from Shades of Noir)

[107] Bertrand Russell, A History of Western Philosophy. (George Allen & Unwin, London, Boston, Sydney. 1961. p.509)

[108] Pierce Penilesse His Suplication To The Divell.(London 1592) ed. McKerrow, I,186

Not only was Italy accepted as decadent but it was also safer for playwrights of the time to transpose action abroad in order to make political comment without danger to their lives. [109]  For example, the social and economic abuses castigated by Vindici in his tirades against usury and against farmers' sons who have decided to become gentlemen are English, and clearly so, typical targets of the satirists of the period.

> " When farmers' sons agreed, and met again, To wash their hands and come up gentlemen;" [110]


## THE LAW - STATE & CHURCH

There was a sense too, that the law served those who could buy it. The reign of James I started and continued in political and economic instability, and a sense of dissatisfaction with the law is inherent in many Jacobean dramatic works.  A topic which reflected popular opinion was also shaded by personal problems with the law on the part of playwrights. Middleton, for instance, suffered at the hands of the law, both through his work and as a result of legal proceedings over his father's estate. *A Game of Chesse*, though rapturously received when performed in 1624 caused Middleton to be summoned before the Privy Council. The play, which was put on day after day, unlike other new plays of its time, and attracted audiences of at least 3000 on each of the first four performances, wildly inflamed the audience against the Spanish, causing the Spanish Ambassador to go into hiding. He complained to James I, and despite the play having been cleared by the Revels Office, the theatre was closed until the company promised not to perform the play again. The actors got off lightly, but it is probable that Middleton was jailed for his more serious part in the actual writing of the play.[111]  In his private life, Middleton had been familiar with the law since his mother's unfortunate remarriage in 1586. This second marriage resulted in several, continued lawsuits between Middleton's mother Anne and her husband Thomas Harvey, between Anne and her son-in-law, Alan Waterer,

---

[109]  Not always successful; see Privy Council re; Middleton

[110]  The Revenger's Tragedy, (II.i.216-7) Usually attributed to Tourneur but many modern scholars  suggest Middleton as author of this work.

[111]  Thomas Middleton, Richard Hindry Barker, (Columbia University Press, New York, 1958.p.21

and between Anne, Waterer and Harvey.[112]  It is possible that this background also strongly coloured Middleton's attitude to women.

A condemnation of the clergy for self-interest is another theme common to many Jacobean plays. Una Ellis-Fermor says the times held "a mood of spiritual despair"[113] and there would seem to be much dissatisfaction with the church who preached damnation as the price of knowledge and power yet lined their own pockets and indulged themselves in many vices. The Catholic Church was seen as the greatest threat, with the power of the church linked to the struggle to seize political power all over Europe. *The Cardinal*, [114] brings to a climax a series of plays, perhaps beginning with *The Duchess of Malfi* [115] , which dealt with the corruption, ambition and sexual indulgence of the clergy. It is perhaps indicative of the times that *The Cardinal* ends with the destruction of all that is good. Other plays, whilst having a mainly historical setting, also feature the clergy in roles of opposition. *Perkin Warbeck* [116] , written just before the civil war when a weak and autocratic monarch nearly brought England to disaster, features in a minor role, an ineffectual king, in a secondary role, an aggressive militarist and in a dominant role a hated ecclesiastic; managing at once to criticise both regimes of state and church.[117]

In film noirs this disillusionment with the law often manifests itself as a lone private detective operating on the side of truth but up against the judicial system. The noir detective hero is most often private, although sometimes he can be the one good cop in a barrel of bad ones. He must operate on the fringes of the law, at once on the side of the law and the criminal, part of both worlds, yet belonging to neither. He operates in a nether world, a world of shadows, where truth is neither black nor white. He often operates against a corrupt system, but may operate against a blind one for, as I have mentioned, truth and justice often run on parallel lines. It is also interesting to note the re-emergence of the gangster film in the fifties. Where before, in the thirties, the gangsters had been mainly concerned with fighting

---

[112] Ibid. p.2-6

[113] The Jacobean Drama

[114] The Cardinal, James Shirley, 1641

[115] The Duchess of Malfi, Webster

[116] Perkin Warbeck, John Ford, 1641

[117] Jacobean & Caroline Tragedies, ed. R.G. Lawrence, Everyman's University Library (J.M.Dent & Sons, London. 1974. p.8)

prohibition, later films portrayed them involved in syndicated crime. There is a return to the theme of the power of money to corrupt, which the Jacobeans were very familiar with. The thematic circle is completed by recent noirs like *The French Connection* but with the shift from illegal alcohol to today's equivalent, drugs. There is still an Italian link as well, with the Mafia connection running throughout.

In *Cracker* there is never the suggestion that the law is corrupt, but very often it is blind because of the prejudices or weaknesses of its officers. There is the assumption of guilt and the reaction to this, for example the arrest of Kelly in *The Mad Woman In The Attic*

> AS SOON AS THEY'RE CLEAR, BILBOROUGH PULLS OFF THE COAT. BECK'S FACE IS RIGHT UP AGAINST KELLY'S. BECK GRABS HIM BY THE THROAT...
> BECK: (HORRIFIC, VIOLENT) "Right, you perverted, murdering bastard, now's the time to start talking. Right ? Now's the time to start talking..."
> BILBOROUGH: (COOL, RATIONAL, ALL PART OF THE ACT) "Leave him.. Leave him. I trust this man so just leave him, okay ?"
> BECK: "...cause I'm gonna smash your face through the glass... I had a niece that age. That could've been my niece you butchered..."
> BILBOROUGH: "Not yet, Leave him for now. That's an order. Okay ?"
> BECK: "... you sick twisted gobshite..."
> BILBOROUGH: "Now listen, you're finished. You're gonna be remanded. You know what that means ? for someone like you ? Hundreds of blokes just like him, all wanting to get at you, all wanting to cut your balls off because they think you're a beastie..".[118]

While Beck voices the feelings of the masses directly, because he shares them, Bilborough expresses them in a more rational manner. Both, however, are evidence of how easy it is to make our own fears into a mantle of guilt for the accused. Bilborough will act just as irrationally when he insists on Cassidy's guilt in *One Day A Lemming Will Fly*, despite Fitz telling him he is mistaken. Beck, of course, shows many weakness throughout *Cracker* culminating in his rape of fellow officer Jane Penhaligon, but that act is outside the scope of this book.

---

[118] Sc.50A. p.67-68

## Violence

Beck & Kelly in the police car after Kelly's arrest. "Right you perverted, murdering bastard ..."

## Mirrors - leading to the truth

Will Fitz see the truth about Kelly in the mirror ?

Fitz finds a due to the murderer's identity behind the bathroom mirror.

## The monastery

The castellated towers offer security from the world

The high shot as Fitz & Penhaligon leave Kelly at the monastery signifies resolution.

# PART TWO - STRUCTURE AND THEME

## PARALLEL PLOTS

Parallel plots form an important part of *Cracker's* structure. From the beginning Gub Neal and his team felt it imperative that the crime story should affect the private story, that Fitz should react to the crimes and people he had to deal with and this in its turn should affect the way he behaved. Catriona McKenzie told me, "its the writer's job to create the characters but Gub, as producer, had control over the feel of the piece, so that's where Gub thinking about Jacobean tragedy and stuff like that comes in. Although people probably didn't sit down in a room and discuss it, you'll feel that influence pervading it."[119]

When Neal suggested to McGovern that he read *The Changeling*, McGovern found "the idea that Gub recommended it interesting" but says, "it didn't influence me one bit."[120] . But then, as Wilson told me, "he went and did it." [121] I believe Neal hoped to draw attention to the parallel plots in the play, rather than suggesting storylines McGovern might follow. Written by Middleton and Rowley in 1622, *The Changeling* is a story of how men makes fools of themselves for love. Whilst the main plot concerns the tragic course to damnation embarked on by Beatrice and her lover De Flores, who kills twice for her, the sub-plot is an ironic tale of Antonio who has himself committed as a madman in order to be near to his love, the young wife of the asylum jailer. Sadly the subject of the title, the true changeling, was cut from the most recent television adaptation of *The Changeling*, along with the entire sub-plot, making a mockery of the play. [122] Even the superb performance of Bob Hoskins as De Flores could not compensate for the desecration wrought on the script. In addition to the device of 'men who make fools of themselves for love', though lust might be a more accurate word for the passions both men display, there is the parallel in reverse for their female counterparts. Joost Daalder suggests that the sub-plot contains a sane woman in a madhouse and the main plot an insane woman in a

---

[119]  Authors interview, 2.2.96.
[120]  Letter, 1994
[121]  Authors interview, 30.11.95.
[122]  BBC2, 11.12.93.

sane world. [123]  Beatrice is not so much insane as unable to deal with her sexual desire in a sane manner, she is overtaken by her passions, which she does not admit to, let alone try to understand. McGovern may say the play did not influence him at all, but it contains themes he is very familiar with; love, passion, adultery, envy, jealousy, guilt and murder. After all, every tragedy has to end in a bloodbath whether it was written in 1593 or 1993.

Other Jacobean plays have parallel lines of action which echo each other. For example in *The Revenger's Tragedy* [124] the relationship of Ambitioso and Supervacuo to their younger brother Junior is remarkably similar to the relationship of Vindici (the Revenger of the title) and his brother Hippolito to their sister Castiza. Vindici and Hippolito are loyal to each other but lead one another into a course of action ending in death. They would protect Castiza's honour but behave as if they would corrupt her. Ambitioso and Supervacuo bungle their attempt to save Junior from prison and cause his execution instead. Later in the play they consider using their rapiers to end the dishonour caused by their mother's incestuous lust for Spurio while Vindici and Hippolito bring their mother out with daggers in their hands preparing to purge her of her dishonour in being bawd to her own daughter. [125] At the end of the play the author lets parallels give way to fusion by showing that Vindici and Hippolito drive to transform an evil court into a good one ends by violent means in the same way as Supervacuo and Ambitioso drive to overthrow the state and gain power for themselves.  *The Revenger's Tragedy* is also a good example of family relations being 'out of joint', which I discussed earlier. Parallels can also be found in comedy. In *A Chaste Maid in Cheapside* Middleton provided four intrigues all of which are sex triangle of two men and one woman. He also wrote ironically balanced ensemble scenes such as the debased christening in act III and the joyous funeral in act V.

Whilst not remembering any specific mention of Jacobean tragedy at script meetings he is clear that *The Mad Woman In The Attic* several parallels. Firstly there is the dual development of the identity of the suspect, Kelly, and

---

[123]  The Changeling - New Mermaids, introduction,p.xxiv

[124]  Registered in 1607 and attributed to Cyril Tourneur but modern scholars suggest re-assigning authorship to Thomas Middleton.

[125]  Spurio , the Duke's bastard, is only a son by marriage to the Duchess, but in Jacobean times this would have been considered incest.

the detective, Fitz. Kelly, the character played by Adrian Dunbar, is truly the nameless man, we, and Fitz, must not only discover whether he is the killer but also have to uncover his identity. In the process we also discover the identity of Fitz as he reveals himself. This relationship was what Winterbottom found most interesting in the script from the start. "What was really attractive," he says, "was Fitz's character and the quality of Jimmy's writing, the way he made the relationship between Fitz's character and the character played by Adrian work. The whole programme was about the way anyone has the capability to do these terrible things. At the heart of the film were these three big interrogation scenes. What was so interesting about it was those scenes which would usually be fairly predictable and boring, just interludes between the plot, that's where it was all happening. Fitz revealing himself in order to try and catch the other guy out and gradually those two , in the way they related together, became almost friends through trying to force someone to confess to something it turns out he hadn't done anyway."[126] There is something of an air of the confessional in these interrogation scenes where Fitz bares his breast in order to show his sympathy with the suspect and to effect his confession in return. He tries the 'man to man' approach first , telling Kelly ," It's nature. Nature knows. Men have to penetrate women or the species dies, now with all that a t stake do you really think Nature cares how we do it ? Whether we say please or think ? Whether she's willing. Mmm ? Sex crimes; a little of what nature requires taken to excess. Murder too - healthy aggression taken a little to excess. I'm saying I understand you. Yes ? " [127] Understanding is important for the detective and the audience. McGovern is clear that "if you are going to do a series about what drives people to do the things that they do, old conventional crime rules had to go out the window. You have to fully understand the villain, or not fully but certainly have to be on the side of the villain."[128] He remembers a TV series of the late fifties or early sixties called *No Hiding Place* which starred the late Raymond Francis as Inspector Lockhart and admits its influence on his work. "It often tried to explain <u>why</u> the baddies acted as they did. And often I wanted them to get away with it." [129] .Ironically it is Kelly who understands Fitz better, saying to him, "There's a great sadness in your life." and ,"It's you who needs the psychologist"[130] ,

126   Ibid.
127   Cracker - The Mad Woman In The Attic. Final script, sc. 57. p.88
128   Authors interview, 5.2.96.
129   Letter to author, 1994
130   Cracker. Sc.57.p.88.

giving perhaps the first indication that he is not a killer but a man used to dealing with other people sympathetically. Like a priest maybe? Winterbottom says that the dialogue in the interrogation scenes was ,"where you really understood him." When he was talking to the suspect ,"what he was saying about rape, everyone's desire to do these terrible things, it was there he really revealed himself. You saw the consequence of his behavioural problems outside, but there, in the police station, he seemed to be able to say what he liked in order to catch the guy. That's how you would understand what sort of character Fitz was, through what he said to Adrian." [131] It is evident that character development is the key to Winterbottom's work as he describes his approach to *Cracker*, and that most of his 'feelings' for what is right come from his empathy towards the characters McGovern has created. Winterbottom finds his understanding of the script through his understanding of the individual characters and the way they react to one another. He makes decisions about how to shoot a scene based on where a particular character would go, how they would think, what it important to them, why they behave the way they do. In a series where the ' why' and not the 'who' is at the centre of things, Winterbottom is certainly an ideal director to start with. He thinks deeply about things, changing the setting of the scene where Fitz and Judith go out to dinner with friends from a restaurant to a jazz club because it would set the mood for both the kind of character he is and the kind of story which will unfold. The final script still shows the scene set in the Ambassador Restaurant and stage directions give instructions for a "gentle cabaret." Winterbottom's change gave the opportunity to have melancholy jazz sung hauntingly by Carol Kidd, which he then uses throughout the story to emphasise the loss felt by all the characters. Cutting between scenes of the dead girl's parents travelling to the morgue and identifying the body and scenes in the club where Fitz becomes more and more drunk and abusive while the same song flows from one to another gives an eerier link from the chaos caused by death to the chaos caused by Fitz's gambling. Winterbottom says he saw the script clearly setting Fitz collapsing," the final collapse when he realises this person he knows has been killed." McGovern "makes explicit the connection between Fitz's crumbling domestic life, his gambling, drinking and so on, and the chaos he goes to clear up. That kind of irony is heavily marked in the script."[132] McGovern says, "its his turn to pay and he knows there's no

---

[131] Authors interview, 5.2.96.
[132] Authors interview, 5.2.96.

money on his card, and he despises himself. Its self-loathing, it just erupts and he vomits it out. He does it by picking on somebody and he picks a very easy target. That's pretty mundane bourgeois hypocrisy, not a great evil."[133] It is not a great evil, but is the final straw which will make Judith walk out , "after a lifetime of suffering," taking the only thing of importance to her, their daughter Kate. This gives us another parallel; the Appelbys have lost a daughter, murdered by the serial killer and now Fitz loses a daughter through his sin. The next morning we discover a further loss for Fitz, the loss of a symbolic 'daughter', as he realises he knew the dead girl who was one of his students. This symbolic father-daughter relationship is underlined later when we see Fitz recorded on video tape with the girl, a tape Fitz apparently knows the contents of.  Ann Appelby tells Fitz, "I'll leave him. When it's all over and she's buried." "Why ?" asks Fitz. "It's what she wanted. I'll leave you then." [134] There is a sense of the mother knowing that her daughter found in Fitz, her professor, a replacement for her own father who she felt inadequate, and a sense of her understanding of Fitz's fondness for the girl and his need to grieve amongst her possessions. This is how McGovern and Winterbottom build up the story, by casting insights into their players. Winterbottom found the way the story allows us to give an identity to 'the suspect' and 'the girl' fascinating, yet another parallel in the plotting. "We start with this nameless man," he says, "which is great for the first episode. It's a blank which Fitz projects onto, he almost persuades us he (Kelly) is the terrible character he creates. We only see Kelly through Fitz. Adrian sits and does hardly anything while Fitz has pages and pages. That's what made it interesting.... There are stories like it all over the papers and the TV, but the way Jimmy handled it, started with a corpse, treated it like a corpse, the reason to start the investigation, something you don't really think about. Then seeing  the mother's reaction , then finally seeing her alive on tape with Fitz. You start with a body and end with someone alive rather than the other way round. You start with a cold thing but it ends up making you feel and understand how people feel about her.  It's good to be heartless at the beginning in order to try and show that."[135]  You see why the scenes of Kelly's arrest are so brutal, why the hospital and the police station have to be stark, empty, lonely, just as the morgue is. Kelly and Jacqui are both unknown to us at the beginning but our sympathy for the suspect and victim

---

[133]  Authors interview, 5.2.96.
[134]  The Mad Woman In The Attic,  final script, sc.66.p.100
[135]   Authors interview, 5.2.96.

is allowed to develop as we begin to piece together a picture of their identities. In the end the identity of the <u>real</u> killer is incidental except in his function to provide narrative closure, allowing the audience to see justice done, Fitz to prove his worth and the mother to grieve for her daughter. She can not do this without the arrest of the killer saying, "I want to grieve for my daughter. I can't because he is standing between us. He's in the way and I want him out of the way forgotten. I want to be able to grieve." [136] Winterbottom describes the crime as, "quite predictable", and the killer "a necessary evil" emphasising his attitude to the areas of the story of most importance to him; the relationship between the suspect and Fitz and the parallel relationship of the victim and Fitz.

Wilson was also aware of parallels in his story, *To Say I Love You,* and suggested that it contained several examples of direct parody and satire. Sean is arrested for stealing a bus at the same time as Fitz is arrested for ringing on hid father-in-law's door for too long and harassing Judith, his wife and, Wilson says, "there were direct mirrors as you went through" the story.. [137] The idea that Sean could not express himself in words because of his stutter mirrors the idea of Fitz being unable to express himself in his marriage. Wilson also felt that the "sort of love scene" where Fitz gets Giggs and Penhaligon to re-enact the murder at the scene of the crime also mirrored the murder. He re-shot some of the day scene, where Fitz and Penhaligon re-enact the murder, after shooting the night scene, having marked the floor with exact positions for the actors and used exactly the same camera positions for both scenes. Giggs makes lewd grimaces at Penhaligon which she receives in good humour, but Wilson has Fitz in Sean's place raising an imaginary weapon over Giggs head. This not only signifies Fitz jealousy and desire to posses Penhaligon for himself which Wilson makes clear with a shot of Fitz and Penhaligon mirroring Sean and Tina after the murder, but signals the death of Giggs. In the murder of Giggs, Wilson places Sean behind him , this time raising a metal pipe, in a shot composed exactly as the ones earlier where Sean kills Cormack and Fitz pretends to kill Giggs. He says tried to mirror throughout, "In compositions and everything, I was mirroring all the time, that was a very key word. When I read the script, I thought 'I like the way the sub plot

---

[136] The Mad Woman In The Attic, sc.42.p.62.
[137] Authors interview, 30.11.95.

Night - Cormack & Tina embrace

Day - Giggs & Penhaligon embrace

Night - Cormack & Tina kiss

Day - Giggs & Penhaligon

Night - Sean kills Cormack

Day - Fitz 'kills' Giggs

Night - Sean makes love to Tina

Day - Fitz 'makes love' to Penhaligon

mirrors the main line'. " [138]  In the original script McGovern wrote a scene where Fitz symbolically smashes a mirror in the casino in order to get himself banned.[139] Unfortunately this symbolic action was lost in filming, with Fitz merely overturning a gaming table instead. It is, however an act signifying Fitz inability to stop gambling willingly as he is unable to face his problems;   in other words, he can not face himself. This is despite Judith leaving him because of his gambling saying as she left, "Why not a normal addiction, Fitz ? Heroin or cocaine - do too much and you're dead ? Why pick something so bloody limitless ?" [140]  There are other parallels in *To Say I Love You* with an element of irony or parody. Penhaligon's revelation to Fitz about his marriage being at an end, followed by his ride home in a taxi immediately precedes the murder of Giggs and his final ride in a car. Both driving sequences are through the dark city streets, and evoke a very noir mood. The stage directions read,

> ON FITZ, THE LIGHTS OF THE CITY SLIDING BY. HIS WORLD
> HAS FALLEN APART...[141]

 Fitz believes his life has come to an end, Giggs life, meanwhile, has literally come to an end.

The idea of ironic parallels continues in *One Day A Lemming Will Fly*. At the beginning of the story Fitz is unable to make love to Judith who has by now returned home. He leaves their bed and goes to the casino, where he catches the croupier trying to cheat him. To punish him, for telling on the croupier, but also for leaving his marital bed, he is beaten up on his way home. Meanwhile a couple have their illicit lovemaking in a wood interrupted by the discovery of a boy's body.  The theme is that love making, that is to say, sexual intercourse, is not possible. This also mirrors the main story of illicit love; Cassidy loved the dead boy but could not admit to it, the boy felt rejected by Cassidy, his parents, his brother and his peers.  Bilborough is also unable to make love to his wife as she is having a baby, so while he still loves, her he cannot express his love physically, just as Fitz, Cassidy and the couple were unable to consummate their feelings. The boy's parents are also split, they "rowed over Tim, separated over Tim," the father hoping for a

---

[138]  Ibid.
[139]  Sc. 85. p.177
[140]  The Mad Woman In The Attic, sc.29. p.39
[141]  SC.89. .189

Night - in the alley - Sean raises
the brick to strike Cormack from
behind while he embraces Tina.
Sean is angered by Cormack's
activity.

Day - in the alley - Fitz re-enacts the
murder, raising his hands behind
Giggs while he embraces
Penhaligon. Fitz is jealous of Giggs
easy relationship with Penhaligon.

Night - at Tina's flat - Sean strikes
Giggs from behind with a length of
pipe when he comes to have sex with
Tina. Sean is angered by Giggs
presence.

crisis to bring them back together. Ironic then, that the crisis he wished for is the death of Tim, the cause of the problem. Even Tim's brother, Andy, feels guilty that he never showed his love for his brother for fear his friends should think he was "a poof" too.

To sum up, one might say that the first *Cracker* story is about loss of faith, the second is about inability to communicate and the third about the impossibility of putting feelings into practice; thought, word and deed.


MOOD

I have already suggested that the writing of *Cracker* partly sets its mood through its story, usually a murder investigation, and style, the way the dialogue develops between protagonists. I now wish to concentrate on the visual elements which arise from a reading and treatment of the script, and which create its ambience and mood. .

*Cracker*, like most Jacobean tragedy and film noirs, has a city setting which sets much of the mood of the piece. Wilson says, "film noir is about urban situations. It's very simple. Even when it's set in the country side, it's about urban situations, about disenfranchised people, gangsters, working class people, wrestlers, boxers, whores, hookers, the drama of urban tragedy. And *Cracker's* an urban drama, so it's bound to be like film noir, there's no question." For economic and logistical reasons *Cracker* was filmed in Manchester, the home of Granada Television, but designer Chris Wilkinson thought the setting very appropriate to the series anyway. He remembered a series called *Bulman*, which started life as "The XYY Man", filmed in downtown Manchester some time ago. Manchester at that time was very gothic, looming, with dark shadows and, although the city has changed a lot, Wilkinson wanted to make *Cracker* have the same dark mood. He was able to recreate the gothic feel of the old police station, making his set seedy and dark, which gives the long interrogation scenes a bleak, stark feeling and creates a sense of desolation and despair. Wilkinson tried to keep as many locations as gloomy as possible, with the exception of Fitz's house where larger rooms made the filming of multiple scenes easier. Even then he used colour to help create mood, dark blue for Mark's room where he broods alone for much of the first series, yellow in the kitchen to give a lighter feel to family scenes. Frederic Jameson found that places often act as characters or 'actants' in film noir. There is, "a kind of architectural language" and "people match their spaces," also finding that colour followed "people and their spaces."[142]

Wilkinson says that the dark mood "was played even heavier" in *To Say I Love You* because of the story. Sean and Tina's flat was filmed at the Hulme development, blocks of flats built in the 1960's, which was knocked down just after *Cracker* was finished. Wilkinson told me, "they were built on ideals, like Corbusier, but they all leaked, it was a disaster, they all became squats."[143] Which, of course, made them very appropriate for *Cracker*. Wilkinson was disappointed that the "castellated house" they found for the monastery had not been featured more as it really gave the idea of Kelly retreating to a castle or fortress, shut in from the outside world. Wilkinson also told me they had to find old railway stock for *The Mad Woman In The Attic* as the "new was too clean, too bright. We wanted saturated colours, browns and ochres." He was inspired by the Hopper painting *Nighthawks* , where it's "dark outside, bright inside." David Piper says, "Hopper's realistic vision" is "convincing as a statement of the condition of twentieth-century man". [144] In *Nighthawks* the harsh interior is contrasted by the sombre exterior, a man sits at the milk bar with his back to us, the white-coated attendant serves a couple who sit apart, not communicating. It is a three o'clock in the morning painting, at any moment Bogart might walk in or turn around. If there ever was such a thing as a noir painter, Hopper was it. Other works show a similar isolation of characters and a severity of light, contrast between colours or black and white, shadows falling across streets; evoking a mood that Wilkinson, with the help of cinematographer Ivan Strasberg, recreated in *Cracker*. Hopper's works are not shown in colour here but his paintings can be seen in many galleries and reproductions viewed easily online on various websites.

---

[142] Shades of Noir - The Synoptic Chandler (Shades of Noir, ed. Joan Copjec) p.37
[143] Authors interview, 26.1.96.
[144] The Illustrated History of Art, W.H. Smith Exclusive Books, p.454-455. Piper gives a biography of Hopper as well as a critique of his work. Illustrations are, Nighthawks, The Automat, Night Shadows, Approaching a City.

## LIGHT & COMPOSITION

Light is a feature of both design and cinematography and is probably the most important element in conveying mood because of its instant impact on the eye and the symbolic connotations it holds. In film noir it is most often chiaroscuro lighting which first suggests a mood of impending doom, a place and time of dark deeds. Barry Norman says, "What tells you immediately that you're watching a film noir is the lighting. It's dark and shadowy, hinting at mystery, and this impression is often heightened by the fact that the scenes are shot at night." [145] Wilson suggests, urban deeds can take place anywhere, and it if often the absence of light, a shadow falling across a face which signals that all is not well. The use of light and dark to signify good and evil is as old as the world, ancient civilisations worshipped the sun as giver of life or made sacrifices to the gods of darkness to make them more tolerant.

In Elizabethan and Jacobean writing the sun, moon and stars were all symbols of good, and symbolic relationships between men's eyes and the macrocosm of sun. moon and stars common. The sun could be the eye of God, eyes contrasted with stars, eyes representing active life, stars the completative, or sun and moon symbols of eyes to the soul. Commonly used was the metaphor linking cosmic darkness, depriving the outward eye of proper light, with darkness of the soul. For instance the world transformed into hell is "defect of light" until a "flaming torch" is put into the poet's hand in *The Transformed Metamorphosis*.[146] The use of torchlight is used symbolically to show evil, i.e. the false light of torches in place of the true light of the sun, moon and stars. The symbolic use of light, or day, for good, dark, or night, for evil has found its way through popular literature as well as drama. Chandler acknowledges it in the introduction to his collected works,

> "Possibly it was the smell of fear which the stories managed to generate. Their characters lived in a world gone wrong, a world in which, long before the atom bomb, civilisation had created the machinery for its own destruction and was learning to use it with all the moronic delight of a gangster trying out his first machine gun. The law was something to be manipulated for profit and power. The streets were dark with something more than night." [147]

---

[145]  Barry Norman, Radio Times, (14-20th Oct. 1995, p. 58)

[147]  Raymond Chandler, The Chandler Collection, Vol. three, p.9

*Nighthawks* - Hopper, 1942

*The Automat* - Hopper, 1927

*Nighthawks* provided inspiration for *Cracker* designer Chris Wilkinson but much of Ivan Strasberg's lighting echoes the colour composition in Hopper's paintings as well. Suggesting an air of urban isolation and loneliness, Hopper explored themes, composition and light also found in film noir. Similarities to his work can be found throughout *Cracker* series one.

*Approaching a city* - Hopper, 1946

*Night shadows* - Hopper, 1921

In film noirs sets are very often lit by artificial light; the detective or heroine entering a darkened room only lit by the narrow beam of their pocket torch, the beams of a car's headlights dimly lighting the highway or street, the glimpse of gunfire through a chink in the blind. While torches signify 'artificial' light and thus 'danger' and the need for caution, one might also see them as 'bringer of light' when wielded, like a magic sword, by the hero or heroine. When interiors are well lit they are often brash, like the milk bar in 'Nighthawks painted by Edward Hopper in 1942, and figures isolated by their size and position within the frame. In daytime decors monumentalism is common, the human figure tiny in a deserted spot, a huge building, a staircase, where space and light can be played on simultaneously. Expressionist lighting gives rise to figures illuminated by a minimum of light so, on a moonless night, our hero is lit by neons, flashing outside his seedy office windows or flickering in alleys. Buildings are often invisible, lights placed low setting a dark space to indicate the absence of sun or moon. Light is partial, placed next to the camera it isolates the figure in white against a black background, placed behind the figure it creates a silhouette against a black background, placed laterally it delineates the silhouette by maintaining zones of shadow. Another characteristic is the absence or weakness of fill light, creating dense shadows on one side of the frame. These shadows indicate a nocturnal aspect while the rest of the frame can be violently lit. Marc Vernet suggests this type of expressionist lighting can be found in real exteriors of Italian films of the 1950's and 1960's in addition to film noir. [148] Michael Winterbottom lists Italian films of this period among the influences on his work. There is a sense of artificial light representing not good but deception, things out of place. The flickering lights can be seen as symbols of the hero's position on the boundary between good and evil, his ability to move between two worlds. The hero's position half in light and half in dark is also symbolic of his place between night and day, good and evil, danger and safety.

There are consistent and frequent examples of expressionist or noir lighting in *Cracker.* At the beginning of the first episode, Fitz is backlit by a white screen, which dominates the frame, in the university lecture theatre. [149] The parallel lines of lights in the ceiling which we see as he throws the textbooks

---

[148] Film Noir on the Edge of Doom, p.9
[149] See Citizen Kane, Orson Welles, Mercury, (1941), for a similar shot.

are reminiscent of lights in the street, or car headlights zooming before our eyes. The composition of the scene at the mortuary echoes the shot of Fitz backlit at the university. Winterbottom makes use of available light from cars to light Fitz and Judith on their way home from the jazz club, the diminishing light signifying the darkness about to enter Fitz's life. A scene where Fitz travels on the tram is also lit only by neons, car lights and shop fronts. A bluey-green glow pervades the scene and the inspector who asks for Fitz's ticket peers menacing at him from the shadows. When Bilborough questions Kelly in hospital, the detective is backlit while Kelly remains in shadow, later, in the interrogation room the dirty green paintwork is lit brashly giving a feeling of sickness. At the dog track the scene is again lit by available light, a mixture of blue and green gives the same feelings of unease just before Kelly is attacked. When Fitz and Kelly set off on their ill-fated journey to find Kelly's wife, we see the city lit by its lights, gleaming like false stars outside the train carriage. Finally, when Fitz and Penhaligon set off to catch the murderer, they emerge from the darkness of the police underground car park into bright sunlight; we know their mission will be successful. The lights of the city in the opening shot of *To Say I Love You*, immediately signal an urban setting, a story of night people. This is reinforced as we enter the pub and find ourselves in a world of shadows. Wilson uses monumentalism to emphasise the feelings of isolation Sean and Tina experience, making them tiny figures against the looming bulk of the block where Tina lives. He uses the same technique to make Fitz seem small against the backdrop of buildings when he waits to confront Graham, Sean is made into a small figure in the city streets as he goes to kill Sammy, and the story ends on a shot of Penhaligon and Fitz embracing, crouched in the road, a small focus of harmony in the midst of a world turned to chaos. Once we enter the haven of Tina's personal world, small table lamps, and later candlelight, suggest that, here at least, Sean and Tina find refuge from the outside horrors. We are reminded of the fragility of this refuge when Cormack and his bullies smash into the flat. By shooting from inside Judith's wardrobe, Wilson makes evil silhouettes out of the clothes Fitz has bought with his winnings, making us share Judith's rejection of them. When Tina first visits her parents we are deceived into thinking it is good by the placement of Sean and Tina outside in the dark while warm light glows inside the house. It is, however, a false light, signifying Sean and Tina's isolation from her family. Once inside the house, Tina's parents are lit strangely from either side of the camera. Evil shadows make her mother look like the wicked Mrs

1. City streets lit only by headlights.

2. The city barely illuminated by artificial light.

3. City streets lit by the moving lights of the tram.

4. Fitz provides his own light on the dimly lit tram.

Fitz & Penhaligon leave the dark of the underground police station car park for the light outside - this movement from dark to light signifying their quest for the murderer will be successful.

The soft natural light of dawn contrasts strongly with the brash artificial light inside the station.

1. Fitz is framed small in front of a monumental screen. The composition references a scene in *Citizen Kane* where journalists watch newsreels about Kane.

2. The use of back lighting makes an ominous silhouette of Fitz. This technique was used frequently in expressionist works and film noir to create a sinister feeling.

3. The parallel lines of ceiling lights echo those in Hopper's painting, *The Automat.* They create a flight path for the text books Fitz hurls like game birds over the students heads.

4. Fitz removes his glasses to talk about how he rehearsed his father's death. Perhaps he will turn out to be the murderer ?

5. The stained glass window is used to provide the same silhoutte as before. On the soundtrack, Carol Kidd sings hauntingly "hush little baby don't you cry," as Mrs. Appelby talks soothingly to her dead daughter as if her words can bring her back to life.

1. At the hospital Bilborough is backlit - he belongs to the light.

2. Kelly belongs in the dark, a shadow falls across him. No-one knows his identity, including himself, or if he is the killer.

3. At the police station, Fitz is lit as Bilborough was before.

4. A shadow, darker than before, marks Kelly as a likely suspect.

5. At the racetrack an ominous greenish light signals Kelly is in danger.

Danvers in *Rebecca* and her father a foul accomplice. This lighting is echoed at Judith's parents house; Fitz waits outside in the shadows while inside her father, lit by a standard lamp identical to the one at Tina's parents, makes him an evil twin of her father. The Oedipal threat is clear. The strange gothic lighting at Tina's parents is emphasised by the presence of birds. Designer Chris Wilkinson told me that Wilson had asked for this Hitchcockian touch, reminiscent of both *Psycho* and *The Birds*, where birds are linked to imminent death.[150] Wilson places a false light in the hands of Fitz enemy, the policeman who arrests him holds a torch and Fitz places himself outside the comforting lights of his house when he reaches an all-time low. The alley where the murder takes place is naturally dark, but the placement of light to the edge and rear of the shot serves to emphasise that this act is taking place on the fringe of civilisation. Tina also lures Giggs out of the light and into the shadows of her flat before Sean batters his head in, appearing from the darkness behind his victim as before. Giggs blindness to his peril is underlined by Tina's symbolic blinding of him, first covering his eyes with her hand, then telling him to close his eyes; he complies, sealing his doom.

This is linked to Sammy's blindness. In *To Say I Love You* Tina's sister is blind, and it is this blindness, or lack of light, which starts Tina's problems. Tina becomes sick of seeing for her sister, of describing everything she sees to Sammy. She tells Fitz, "I was born to be a dog." [151] In a later scene Tina even barks at her parents when they are brought to see her, pretending to be the guide dog she thinks she has had to be. Mirroring this is Fitz reaction to the dog belonging to Judith's parents, and Sean's reaction to the dog on the steps of the flats. When Fitz goes to collect his daughter, Kate, the dog, on guard like the dog at Tina's parents house, barks at him; Fitz bares his teeth and growls in return. Sean reacts to the dog in his scene in a similar way; Tina is scared of it but Sean demonstrates his masculine power, as Fitz does, by growls at it. All three dogs are symbols of paternalistic law which is a threat to Tina as a femme fatale, but which can be combated against by Sean and Fitz the tragic and detective heroes respectively. Wilson plays this imagery further, placing a small terrier on the lap of a woman in the bus stolen by Sean and Tina. The dog sits quietly until

---

[150] For a deeper analysis of symbolism in Hitchcock see 'Hitchcock - In Search of a Proper Sense of Id - Entity', Authors essay Derby University, 1994.
[151] To Say I Love You, sc. 146. p.307

The intimate lighting in Tina's flat is in direct contrast to the bleak world outside, she has tried to create a 'home', a refuge. However, her use of candles and disguise of artificial light sources with drapes suggests she is not a stranger to duplicity.

Fitz shares a light with Sean and then Tina when they are in police custody. Each time his action suggests sympathy with the protagonists and signifies Fitz's ability to pass from one world to another, much as the private detectives in film noirs do.

1. Judith's father is backlit to create a forbidding paternalistic figure.

2. Tina's father is lit in the same way, note the same lamp shade. The birds fore grounded, as phallic symbols, signify danger for Tina.

3. Fitz waits outside in the dark at Judith's parents.

4. Sean waits outside in the dark at Tina's parents.

5. The policeman's 'magic' torch finds Fitz the criminal causing a disturbance at Judith's parents.

6. Sean sees Sammy's silhouette in her bedroom window.

7. Fitz feels more at home in the dark. Like an unruly child, he behaves in the way expected of him.

the siren in the police car chasing the bus being to whine; now the dog barks signifying unison with the law. [152] The shot of the terrier barking is bisected horizontally by a bar, which echoes the shot of the three magistrates sitting behind the barrier of their podium in court where Sean appears the following morning. Cerberus, the dog who guards the gate to hell is usually depicted as having three heads, further emphasis of Wilson's use of the dog as a symbol of the Law. One might also consider Kelly's inability to 'see' who he is, his loss of memory, a signifier of what he refuses to 'see', or remember, the murder on the train. His inability to see is signified by the girl's blood which drips in a curtain down the mirror in the train carriage in a similar way to rain running down windows in film noirs; her blood obscures his ability to 'see' the truth. Strangely it is a mirror which gives away the murderer in *The Mad Woman In The Attic*. Fitz finds a cut-throat razor in the bathroom cabinet, which has a mirror on the front, almost shouting "look here !" In another scene, where Fitz borrows £5 from Penhaligon, he can look nowhere, neither can Penhaligon meet his gaze. It is as if both refuse to see the symbolism inherent in the exchange of money which is a reversal on the action in the following scene, where Giggs expects to pass money over to a prostitute. In the final story Fitz is also ritually blinded, being struck over the left eye when he leaves the casino. This signifies his inability to see Cassidy's innocence until it is to late.

Tina emerges from darkness when she is place within a cell, the harsh light making the white tiles gleam like mirrors. There is no possibility of shadows here. Sean, meanwhile, is still outside in the dark. At the end, Sean destroys himself in a burst of false light, the fire from the explosion he causes with petrol. Sean also uses the box of matches as a symbol of his power. Because Sammy cannot see, he shakes the box next to her ear to frighten her, before pushing her face down onto the gas cooker so she can smell the gas he has turned on. When Fitz arrives, Sean twice holds the box of matches up to him, first closed, then open with a match ready to strike. The fact that he cannot use the match while Fitz is present signifies the detective's superior power and his ability to escape the situation, unlike Sean who is doomed to a tragic end. Wilson also uses the lighting of cigarettes in a noir fashion with symbolism comparable to Neff lighting Keys cigar and Keyes finally lighting Neff's cigarette in *Double Indemnity*.

---

[152] To Say I Love You, sc. 25. p.41. Action not scripted, see McGovern's note "I'll script as much of this as ...." (end of page lost)

1. Tina is afraid of the dog which barks at her and Sean on the stairs outside her flat.

2. Sean demonstrates his potency by baring his teeth and growling at the dog.

1. The dog at Judith's parents house barks a warning to Fitz when he comes to collect his daughter Kate.

2. Fitz demonstrates his contempt for paternal order by baring his teeth and growling back at the dog, just as Sean did.

1. The dog sitting on the lap of the lady passenger on the bus Sean steals only barks, in sympathy with the law, when it hears the police sirens.

2. Notice how the composition of the shot of the three magistrates (the three-headed dog Cerberus) mirrors the shot of the dog on the bus. Both are Sean's enemies.

1. Sammy's guide dog shows its teeth to Tina when she visits her parents new home.

2. Sammy's dog watches Tina all the time. She is a threat to Sammy.

3. Sammy's dog goes to her to keep Tina at bay.

4 & 5. Tina barks at her parents when they come to visit her at the police station. She behaves as though she is the (guide) dog she believes they have made her.

When Fitz is called in to Sean's cell at the police station, he is a fellow prisoner; Fitz lights Sean's cigarette as a sign of friendship, help and being on the same side. When Fitz traps Tina into arrest he does not light her cigarette, she lights her own as a sign of her assumed 'masculine' power, she behaves, as Krutnik would say, as a 'phallic' woman. Later, however, after Tina's arrest, Fitz has to try to encourage Tina to help them find Sean; now he does light her cigarette, in the same way he lit Sean's, as a sign they are working on the same side

*One Day A Lemming Will Fly* also opens with city streets, suggesting night activity. Fitz leaves his bed, unable to make love to Judith and goes to a club, where the green light behind the bar warns of trouble. After catching the croupier trying to cheat, Fitz enters the world of street shadows where the only light comes from the sleazy club sign and an odd street light or two. A gang wait, silhouetted to beat him up, although his first attacker is unseen, coming from off screen to hit Fitz with a traffic cone, symbol of the city. The adulterous couple conduct their love-play in the shadows of a wood, the boy's body fore grounded high in frame above their heads. When the police search the woods in the rain, a policeman finds Tim's shoe with the aid of first, his 'magical' torch, then a lamp. When the woman takes the police to the body the police also discover it with the 'magic' light of their torches. When the police take the shoe to Tim's parents house, really the mother's, lamps burn behind the parents, suggesting that hope of Tim being alive still exists. Later, when Bilborough and Penhaligon come to tell them the body has been found, the room is dimly lit, suggesting a loss, the light having gone out of her life. In contrast Fitz's house is brightly lit in this story, Judith's return permitting happy family scenes in a kitchen lit by sunlight. When Bates is questioned in the interrogation room warm light is allowed to shine into the room from the corridor outside, a suggestion that he can return to the light as he is innocent of murder. When Cassidy is questioned the room tends to be cast with a greenish hue, leaving us wondering about his innocence. A flickering light, from a projector, is used to suggest that Andy, the brother of the dead boy, is not entirely without blame. While he is not guilty of murder he, like Cassidy, could have done something to prevent it.

## Monumental shots

This playful shot marks Penhaligon's move in Fitz's life from 'little sister' to 'femme fatale' The monumental aspect of unzipped jeans behind the nuns points to the subconscious intention underlying Penhaligon's offer to Fitz.

Sean is a tiny insignificant figure against the monumental background of city streets as he sets off to kill Sammy.

## Ironic reversal

1. This composition underlines the unease with which Fitz borrows and Penhaligon lends £5.

2. Even after the exchange of money Fitz and Penhaligon can not look at each other. This situation is another ironic reversal - Penhaligon seeming to 'pay' Fitz for scrubbing her carpet, mirroring Giggs expectation of paying Tina for services rendered.

1. Sean shakes the matchbox so Sammy knows what he intends.

2. Sean holds Sammy's head down so she can hear the gas escaping.

3. Sean tries to threaten Fitz with the matches.

4. He moves closer as Fitz fails to back off.

5. Will Sean strike the match ?

6. The spark from the central heating beats Sean to the draw.

7. Fitz is crucified by the blast.

8. Resolution, again signalled by a high shot. The hero gets his girl - Fitz & Penhaligon embrace.

This story is remarkable for one monumental shot. Fitz is placed small in frame at the base of the tower where Cassidy is ready to jump.[153] Once at the top of the block, we have an overhead shot of Fitz lying and Cassidy sitting on the very edge of the building, it is as if we play God. As Fitz stands and pretends to jump, crying, "Let's fly," Cassidy stands and saves him, both are backlit by strong sunlight, dark figures against a light sky, now, at least we will have no death. Our uncertainty about Cassidy does not abate however and the light around him is shadowy in the scene where he walks through the shopping precinct with Fitz and Penhaligon, just before his arrest, all three figures are vague against the brash lights of the shops behind. There is a question over Cassidy, but also over the relationship between Fitz and Penhaligon who share the shadows. One might consider the smashing of Cassidy's window with the JCB arm, a symbolic act on the part of Tim's father and his friend; they remove the object which lets light into Cassidy's room, his light should be extinguished because they believe he should die. In the final scene of this story we see Fitz small against the backdrop of his house after he lets Penhaligon down, the visual imagery suggesting his petty act but also the importance of Fitz family over his passions. The final shot sees Fitz at once part of and yet separate from his family; he sits at a round table, suggesting circularity of action, he will repeat his mistakes over and over again, next to him is an empty chair, for Penhaligon, Judith sits in a sun lounger, working, Mark swings from side to side in his blue hammock, caught in the halfway house of adolescence, Kate plays happily with a swing ball, her circular movement with the ball echoing her father, though her childhood is innocent while his is wilful.

Strasberg, who won a BAFTA for his cinematography on *Cracker*, likes to use natural light where ever possible. He told me, "I am interested in what light does, and what different light does to mood., how, for instance, the weather affects light. On *Cracker* we were helped by bad weather . I try to use natural light sources, and the poor light in Manchester, as well as the rain and the cold, helped to set the mood of the piece." [154] Strasberg, a South African by birth, studied accountancy before an interest in politics and economics led him to Mozambique. He joined a local film society but was

---

[153] See The Crowd, King Vidor, 1928, for a similar low angle shot. (Extract shown on
A personal journey with Martin Scorsese through American movies, C4, 1995)
[154] Authors interview, May 1994

1. At the casino the green light should warn Fitz of impending danger.

2. The street is lit by neons as the gang lies in wait for Fitz.

3. Fitz is ritually blinded in the attack.

Cassidy also has his light taken away.

1. While there is hope that Tim is alive, a light burns behind his mother.

2. With Tim dead his mother has lost the light in her life.

The warm glow from the corridor signifies that Mr. Bates (unlike his namesake Norman) is not a murderer.

The flickering light from the school projector suggests neither Cassidy nor Andy is entirely free from guilt.

thrown out of the country for "unsympathetic activities"(associating with the Blacks). Arriving in England, his interest in film led him to The London School of Film Techniques where he found "fellow students mostly American draft dodgers". [155] Realising the competition to direct was impossible, he concentrated on photography and later became friends, and worked with, Chris Menges. Strasberg says he owes most of what he knows to Menges, who he admires greatly.

It was fortunate that Strasberg's natural inclination, and his documentary experience, led him to use natural light because there was not a great deal of time for lighting on *Cracker*. Strasberg was subject to the same kind of pressures faced by cinematographers on film noirs . Like so many innovations noir lighting owed much of its conception to wartime economic necessity. Dmytryck says he used "brush lighting - you light the person, you throw a shadow across the back wall and you're lit." When asked why he favoured this lighting style, he answered, "Because it was quicker and cheaper . In 1944 I made *Farewell My Lovely* for $40,000 on a very short schedule - 20 days." [156] *Cracker* was made on a similarly tight budget and schedule as Craig McNeil told me, "the audience expects more, more on screen. Budgets were tight, although we spent more in real terms. We had to save by working faster as well as on post - production. For example, *Sherlock Holmes,* for a one hour episode, had a fifteen day schedule, *Cracker*, for the same hour, only had thirteen days." [157] Money was saved on post - production by editing *Cracker* on Lightworks. Because non-linear editing does not require a print McNeil estimated "costs were ten grand down."[158] It was time rather than money that had to be saved on lighting, although in the end it is time which costs the most money. Strasberg operated the camera as well as lighting *Cracker*, making his task a gargantuan one, but it is fortunate that he did so, for it is his hand which pulls together the sometimes very different styles of the three directors.

 Winterbottom favours a quick cutting style for building up moments of tension; for example the sequence of the train rushing towards us with its high overhead shot, strong verticals, and almost sexual quality in its

---

[155] Ibid.

[156] Barry Norman, Radio Times, (14-20th Oct.1995, p.58)

[157] Authors interview, Nov.1995.

[158] Ibid. McNeil's thankless task of saving money and ensuring Cracker did not go over time or budget earnt him Andy Wilson's title of "most un-favourite person".

*One Day A Lemming Will Fly* -  Fitz prevents Cassidy's suicide

1. Monumental shot. The tower looms over Fitz.

2. Bird's eye view of Fitz & Cassidy on the roof.

3. Fitz tells Cassidy that Tim was murdered.

4. Cassidy realises he has not caused Tim's death

5. "One day a lemming ..."

6. Fitz invites Cassidy to jump with him

7. Cassidy stops Fitz

8. Fitz pulls Cassidy away from the edge.

thrusting movement which is then slashed across by a strong horizontal movement as the train wheels hurl past us at ground level. The camera angles and movement signify and pre-empt the sexual nature of the crime, the slashing of the girl's throat. Scenes of the police checking the train, and later arresting Kelly at the hospital , are shot with a sharp edged crispness which shows Winterbottom's Scorsese influence but are also reminiscent of documentary matter of factness. Strasberg manages to make Wilson's more theatrical style at once claustrophobic and give a sense of isolation, of things being out of joint. One has a sense that the whole of *To Say I Love You* takes place at night, with the exception of the final scene when Sean blows himself up. This is not the case, although the story has many scenes which take place at night or dusk. Wilkinson agreed that much of *Cracker* gave the impression of being shot at night, or that it was raining all the time because "it always rains in Manchester." He suggested at the beginning that "it would be great if it was raining all the time", but it would have been too expensive. However, his theory that it always rains in Manchester may have some truth in it as Strasberg found to his advantage. In Jacobean tragedy rain associated with storms is used as a symbol of evil, for the rain obscures the natural sunlight creating a false night. Lightning often accompanies the rain and is a sign of the Devil. In film noir it is often raining with rain running down windows used frequently; for example, outside Bernstein's office in *Citizen Kane*., and the scene where Marlowe spends the night outside the suspect's house in *The Big Sleep*, where the rain pours down the windows of his car. It is not so much a direct symbol of evil but as if the whole city weeps tears of sadness, it evokes a melancholy, world-weary feeling. Rain is often present in this way in *Cracker,* used at times of despair and sadness. In the first story, it is raining when  Kelly visits the farmhouse and finds the woman who has said she is his wife is lying. In the second story it starts to rain after Sean and Tina have murdered Cormack, and Sean accuses Tina of wanting Cormack to enjoy her body. Rain accompanies both the finding of the corpse in the final story and the sad task of visiting Tim's parents with first his shoe, and then confirmation of his death. Each time the city tries to wash away the wrong.

## _One Day A Lemming Will Fly_ - Families - Failure to communicate

1. Fitz & Judith back together, but still apart.

2. Bilborough & his wife find the baby gets in the way.

The pathologist arrives to confirm the cause of Tim's death inappropriately dressed as Napoleon. "Greefes lift up joys, feastes put down funeralls."
(See The Revenger's Tragedy)

1. Penhaligon waits in vain for Fitz at the airport

2. Judith & her children at home.

3. Fitz's desires are small in comparison to his love for his family Note how the composition reduces Fitz to a tiny figure against his house.

4. The family together but not one. Fitz saves an empty chair for Penhaligon, Judith is absorbed by her work, Mark swings idly from side-to-side, Kate echoes the circularity of her Father.

## *The Mad woman In The Attic* - The railway - verticals & horizontals

1 & 2. Winterbottom uses strong verticals to emphasise movement.

 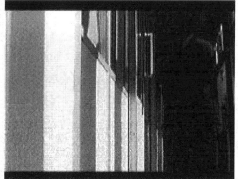

3. A fast horizontal cut slashes like the killer's knife

4. Back to moving verticals inside the train.

 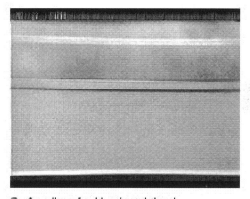

5. The railway lines draw us into the city and the story.

6. Another fast horizontal cut.

7. The railway lines keep the audience on track.

## NIGHT & TRANSFORMATION

The idea of night people is commonly found in film noir, stories often involve people who live by night, singers, nightclub owners, gangsters, or who live a daytime existence in eternal gloom as if they are vampires who will be killed by sunlight. The theme of night and day being "transformed" or inverted is also common in Jacobean tragedy. In *The Revenger's Tragedy* a world of inverted values is depicted, a dark world in which torchlight makes an "artificial noone", [159] and there is a sense that the day is "out ath-socket; that it is noone at Mid-night" [160]

*The Revenger's Tragedy* also shows this transformed world in another way, by the use of masks and disguises. People disguise themselves and dissemble their true intentions and their expectations are transformed by ironic reversals in action and word. Nothing is as it should be, "Time hath sevrall falls. / Greefes lift up joyes, feastes put downe funeralls." [161] There are revells at funerals and revels, when courtiers should masque as virtues, are vehicles for murder and rape. In *One Day A Lemming Will Fly* one scene offers a parody, a kind of reversal where things are out of place. When the pathologist is called in to give a verdict on Tim's death, he arrives at the mortuary dressed for a fancy dress ball, as Napoleon. His disguise, suitable for celebration rather than death, places him as a character unhelpful to the plot. This scene, amended at a late date, may suggest that his evidence is unsound or may merely give an indication that the evidence will lead to the downfall of Cassidy and subsequently Fitz. [162]

Mask is a vehicle for revenge and intrigue, but may have other consequences as well as those intended. For example, in *The Atheist's Tragedy*, [163] Charlemont disguises himself as a ghost in order to torment his enemy D'Amville. Later in the same play, in parallel and parody of Charlemont, Snuffe dresses as a ghost and pursues Soquette around the same graveyard in order to embrace her. Their 'love play' leads Snuffe to embrace the corpse of Borachio by mistake. For Elizabethans and Jacobeans, the primary moral connotation of disguise was evil, the term

---

[159] I.v.33
[160] II.ii.257-8
[161] V.i. 178-9
[162] Sc. 44. p.55-56
[163] Tourneur

being associated with strange apparel, drunkenness, deformity, dissimulation and the devil. The devil, in mediaeval morality plays, was a Vice who rails cynically and disguises himself as a Virtue in order to lead men to damnation. In his true guise the devil was often portrayed as the Vice Revenge, who insists on justice, as in John Pikeryng's play *Honestes* (1597)

The corrupt world, especially the world spawned by the hectic imaginings of Englishmen fascinated by Italy, was commonly represented as 'transformed' in Jacobean literature. For example, Ben Jonson says;

> "Call Divels, Angels; and Sinne, pietie;
> Let all things be preposterously transchanged." [164]

or John Marston's description of Italianate hell,

> " Lorenzo Celso the loose Venice Duke,
> Is going to bed, 'tis now a forward morne
> Fore he take rest. O strange transformed sight,
> When princes make night day, the day there night." [165]

The idea of drunkenness as disguise informs *Cracker* as well as many film noirs. In both there is a hero who disguises himself by drinking to excess, very often to hide from the truth. Fitz's drinking can be seen as further evidence of his need to inflict punishment on himself. He is a clever man who thinks too much and too deeply, it is much easier to hide behind a mask of drunkenness than face reality and have to deal with the consequences. Fitz drunkenness is related to Kelly's amnesia, it is a barrier he puts between himself and the pain of his problems. Noir heroes seem to take refuge in the whisky glass or bourbon bottle as a cure to mend emotional and physical hurts. If a detective is beaten up, he takes his medicine, or it is administered to him by a pretty girl like Carmen in *The Big Sleep*. If a hero's girl leaves him he drowns his sorrows. Fitz turns to the  bottle for comfort whenever he gets the chance, at home, at the club, on the train with Kelly, he even accepts a drink from the murder suspect's father. . His worst exhibitions of drunkenness take place when he feels at his lowest ebb, when he feels most guilty, for example, at the very beginning when Fitz is, "Over the limit on both cards. Two grand overdrawn at the bank," and he has,

---

[164]  Every Man In His Humour, (V.iii.306-7)
[165]  What You Will, (I.i.)

1. Fitz asks Mark if he has been at the scotch.

2. Fitz drains the bottle.

3. Fitz gets very drunk as the meal progresses.

4. Judith drinks tea.

5 & 6. First Fitz drinks alone on the train, but on the return journey, Kelly joins in him drowning his sorrows.

7. Fitz finds solace in the bottle again.

8. Fitz accepts a drink from the murderer's father.

"raised five grand on the mortgage.... I forged your signature."[166] As McGovern says, he picks an easy target to attack, but it is himself he is punishing. In *The Postman Always Rings Twice,* Frank and Cora have to get Nick drunk before they can kill him; their first attempt to electrocute him in the bathroom fails, Nick being protected by the life giving powers of water.


## WATER

Associated with this false cleansing, for alcohol does not wash away problems, it merely hides them, is the true purgative power of water. Fitz, like many noir heroes, for example Philip Marlowe in *The Big Sleep*,[167] turns to the bottle, but there are many instances of its antidote. When he becomes drunk in the jazz club and insults his friends, Jo takes a glass of water and throws it into Fitz's face to cleanse him. The importance of washing and cleansing is underlined by the content of Fitz's tirade; he has criticised his friends for having a black cleaner "with her arm halfway down your lavatory." [168] It is interesting to note that while we see Fitz and his friends drinking alcohol, we see Judith only drinking tea from a cup. This provides a marked contrast to Fitz's over indulgence. We also see Judith refusing to join Fitz in drinking alcohol in *One Day A Lemming Will Fly*.

Bathrooms are important to Fitz. When he learns of the girl's death, he retreats to the bathroom to grieve, shedding copious tears. He also finds the clue about the murderer in a bathroom, finding a cut-throat razor in the mirrored wall cabinet in the Hennessey's bathroom . Fitz very clear reflection of himself in the mirror as he closes the cabinet is a definite signification that he will be successful. Fitz wants to use water to cleanse Mark of his problems, suggesting "a bucket of water" as a solution on finding Mark with his hand down his trousers. In fact, as we discover in *To Say I Love You,* Mark is suffering symptoms of an inflamed appendix which later bursts. Fitz anger is a way of taking out his frustrations, again picking the easiest target to do so.

---

[166] The Mad Woman In The Attic, sc.27. p.36.
[167] Marlowe is played by Humphrey Bogart, Warner Brothers, (1946)
[168] Sc. 26. p.33

1. The fountain of life still flows in the Appelby's garden, they do not yet know of their daughter's death.

2. Jo cleanses Fitz of his sin with a glass of water.

3. Mrs Appelby shares her tears with Fitz.

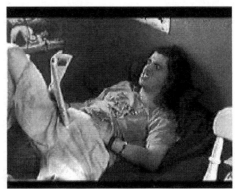

4. Fitz threatens Mark with a bucket of water . In fact his hand is down his trousers to ease the pain of a grumbling appendix, but Fitz assumes something more basic.

5. Rain at the farmhouse .

6. Kelly does still not know who he is.

7. Another body is found in the river.

## Men retreat to the bathroom (toilet) with their problems

*The Mad Woman In The Attic*

1.

2.

3. Fitz cries over the murder of his student (symbolic daughter) Jacqui in his bathroom at home.

*One Day A Lemming Will Fly*

Bilborough hides from his problems at work (the mob waiting to lynch Cassidy) and at home (his pregnant wife) by retreating to the safety of the men's toilet at the police station.

Water is also used as a symbol of life, for example we have seen the 'fountain of life' in the garden outside the dead girl's house, which will be extinguished when they learn of her death. McGovern uses water in a particularly Catholic piece of symbolism in the scene where Kelly cuts himself while peeling potatoes in Fitz's kitchen. Kelly puts his hand under running water from the tap. Not only is the running water a sign of good, the fact that Kelly can place his hand there signifies his innocence, even though the suspense for him and the viewer is prolonged by the placing of a knife in shot with his hand and the water. Which will triumph, the water signifying good or the knife, signifying evil ? The mixing of water and blood is like the celebration of the Eucharist, in which the priest mixes water and wine, the wine substituting for the blood of Christ, perhaps yet another suggestion that Kelly is a holy man and not a criminal..

Tears are another form of running water and therefore a form of purification. Naturally the dead girl's mother cries when Fitz calls to offer help, needing to share her washing away of grief. Her tears in front of Fitz show us that she will allow his help. The chief superintendent also tries to soothe Mrs Appelby by offering her a glass of water in the scene where she is told she will have to ask Kelly for permission to bury Jacqui; it is ironic that he asks Penhaligon to fetch it. Winterbottom films the finding of a second body as an inverse baptism, the police frogmen trawling the river in a parody of Christ's 'fishers of men'. Water has been used to conceal the body but it cannot wash away this mortal sin, it reveals the evil deed instead. Water will not accept the dead body of Giggs either, allowing his murder to be discovered. In film noir bodies often end up 'in the drink', for example in *The Big Sleep*, Marlowe asks if a gun has been found on a corpse fished out of the river the previous day. In *To Say I Love You,* Judith expresses her unhappiness to Fitz by telling him, "Twenty years married to you, I need more than therapy. I need a trip to Lourdes," [169] suggesting she needs the healing waters to take away all her pain and suffering. Meanwhile Fitz drinks his brown drink, symbolic of his unclean attitude to Graham, Judith's therapist and lover-to-be.

The bathroom is also an important place for Sean. We see him wet in the bathroom where his blood will mingle with water when he injures himself during Cormack's attack. After the injury, Tina bathes his wound. While

---

[169] Sc. 9. p. 12

## The healing power of water

*The Mad Woman In The Attic*

1. Kelly's blood mixes with water

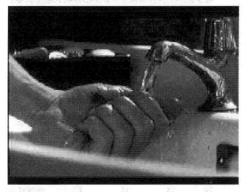

2. Kelly washes under running water

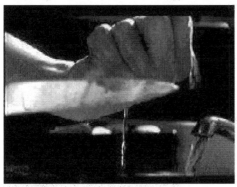

3. Is Kelly the killer ? The knife suggests he may be.

*To Say I Love You*

Fitz's mother tells him to wash away his pain

ILL.25.

*To Say I Love You*

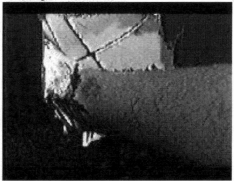

1. Sean cuts his foot

2. Tina bathes Sean's injury

3. Sean cannot wash away Giggs blood

4. Tina bandages Sean's hand

95

Sean is powerless in the bathroom, Tina spits in Cormack's face, first an insult, a sign of her independence, then a signal of her willingness to share her bodily fluids with him in sexual activity. Cormack is aroused and responds by fondling her breast as if to stimulate further flow from Tina, naturally his sexuality will lead to his death  As a symbol of his power as an evil force, Cormack takes Sean's cups from him. These are the symbol of Sean's potence, his masculinity, rewards for his singing which is the only way he can express himself unless he is angry. This act of castration, the taking of the 'cup of life' seals his fate, for now Sean must avenge himself. When Cormack open the door to Tina, he is holding a silver cup like Sean's in his hands, a symbol of the fact he still lives and a reminder of why he is about to die. Ironically, after Cormack's death we see these cups shining like beacons in front of his wife when Penhaligon questions her. The healing power of water is again emphasised when Fitz takes Kate out for the afternoon and they sail on the lake; a still calming, comforting body of water which calms the atmosphere just as Kate calms and restores Fitz. Sean uses water to cleanse him after Cormack's murder, stepping into the shower fully clothed. Wilson uses an overhead shot to show the water pouring down on Sean, cutting to a close up of the plug hole which could be straight out of *Psycho* to show that the water cannot cleanse Sean, he is left with his guilt. After the murder of Giggs Sean sits in the bath unable even to wash, he is so brought down by the weight of his action. Tina's symbolic bandaging of his hand, an echo of her tending his foot at the beginning of the story, is her effort to cleanse him; fist she was Mary Magdalene to his Christ, now she is an ironic Virgin Mary tending her son. Penhaligon attempts a different cleansing when Fitz takes her to dinner at the restaurant where he knows Judith and Graham have gone. As Fitz gets into his usual drunken routine of insults, Penhaligon asks the waiter for, "A large jug of water, with ice," and proceeds to pour its contents over Fitz head. He reacts by making a joke calling it, "Anglo Saxon foreplay," to hide his recognition of is own guilt. After she leaves, Fitz, a realist or fatalist like McGovern, puts the spilt ice in his glass and drinks, perhaps attempting to cleanse himself. Later, after losing at the casino, he does penance by scrubbing Penhaligon's carpet, getting on his hands and knees to remove the dog shit, symbol of his misdemeanour, which he has brought into her flat. This scene, with Fitz doing penance on his hands and knees, strangely mirrors a scene where Fitz visits his mother. This time he does penance for not visiting before by getting on his hands and knees to weed the garden, removing suckers from

1. Tina searches for a knife to stab Cormack.

2. Having failed, she spits in his face.

3. Tina is a defiant femme fatale..

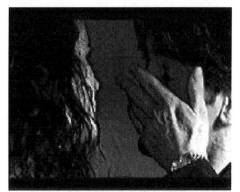

4. Cormack is blinded by Tina's action.

5. Cormack considers Tina's invitation.

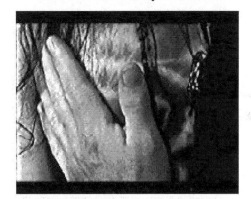

6. Cormack caresses Tina's breast and seals his fate.

7. Tina realises she can control Cormack without the use of a phallic object, all she needs are her feminine powers.

1. Sean gives his prize cup to Tina - symbolic gesture of his male potency.

2. Cormack takes Sean's cups - symbolically castrating him.

3. Sean's cups in Cormack's window act like a beacon to Tina.

4. Cormack strokes a cup when he opens his door to Tina showing both his masculine potency and his power over Sean.

5. Sean's cups gleam triumphantly in Cormack's window as Penhaligon questions his widow.

## The healing power of water

1. Cormack violates Sean's territory.

2. The mirror records Sean's humiliation.

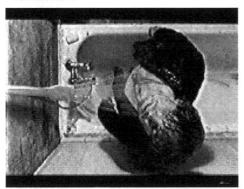

3. The shower washes away Sean's guilt after he has killed Cormack in revenge.

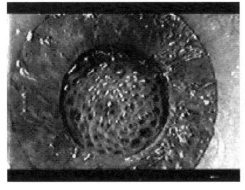

## False liquids

5. Sean drenches himself with petrol, a baptism in reverse for his imminent death.

6. Sean prepares a pyre for Sammy & himself.

7. Sean 'baptises' Sammy with petrol.

4. Cormack's blood mingles with water as it rushes away down a Psychoesque plug hole.

1. Fitz takes his daughter Kate boating on the lake and they play the "what if ...?" game. The still water provides a haven away from Judith's parents house.

2.Sean & Tina run through the rain after the murder of Cormack and their alley-cat love making. The rain seems to wash away all their passion.

3. Fitz waits while Penhaligon goes to look at Giggs corpse which has been found by the canal. The water failed to hide his murder.

4.Sean goes back to the canal to llok at Tina's photo album. He finds the pictures of Tina & Sammy with Sammy scratched out. Even for Sean, water provides a quiet private place to think.

the roses. [170] While he is doing it, a wasp stings his finger and his mother has to tend his wound, this time echoing Tina's treatment of Sean's injuries; strangely, yet symbolically, Fitz's mother tells him to wash his hand under running water to take away the pain. This is yet another indication of Wilson's view of Fitz and Sean as two sides of the story's hero. Fitz on his hand and knees is also used in the final story, Fitz kneeling down next to Judith in the garden when he tells her he is thinking of going on holiday; his penitential position is a sign of his guilt as he plans to go away with Penhaligon.

Penhaligon is allowed to cry twice in *To Say I Love You,* once for Giggs when she tells Bilborough she also cried for her father, and again over Fitz's body when she thinks he is dead. Each time there is a fatherly connection; Giggs, a father and family man is killed, Bilborough has just found out he is to become a father and behaves like a father to Penhaligon in his paternal role as her boss, Fitz is a surrogate father for own dead father. Mark uses liquid as a way of apologising to his father, offering him a cup of tea, a non alcoholic drink and therefore 'good', when Fitz finds small holes in Mark's clothes and suspects him of using drugs. We know Fitz forgives and loves Mark because he is able to cry tears of joy at his bedside in hospital. There is a suggestion of the magical properties of liquid at the forensic laboratory. When Fitz and the police search Giggs's belongings for clues, they stand behind a counter laden with bottles full of coloured liquid. Fitz finds the condom which will give a vital clue to the identity of Giggs's killers. A link back to the alchemy found in Jacobean drama.. False liquid gives Tina away, when she has no hesitation in buying Fitz an expensive drink, he has his suspicions about her confirmed, leading to her arrest. Even Tina is allowed the restorative action of crying when she tells Fitz she was "born to be a dog." One might see the petrol Sean uses to kill himself as a 'false' liquid, particularly as its use results in fire, seen to be the opposite of water. In this story it is Penhaligon who is unable to use the restorative powers of water. Having returned to the police station after recovering Giggs body, Penhaligon finds a spot of blood on the sleeve of her pale yellow jumper. She rubs at it, licks her fingers and rubs again, but it still remains. The spot of blood, like the mark of the virgin bride on her white sheet, is a symbol of her loss of innocence. and marks her passage from the role of 'little sister' to 'femme fatale'.

---

[170] Sc. 58. p.110-111

1. Fitz meeting with Judith is unsuccessful

2. Fitz's 'brown' drink

3. Fitz is made small by having to make peace with Graham

4. Fitz & Graham talk 'man to man' over a drink.

5. Fitz buys Penhaligon a drink before taking her to dinner.

6. Penhaligon washes away Fitz's sin after he uses her as part of his insult to Judith & Graham.

7. Humiliated & small again, Fitz puts the ice from the water jug into his drink.

8. Tina gives herself away by buying Fitz an expensive drink.

Mothers & sons - *The Mad Woman In The Attic* -
The Hennessy house is full of images of mothers & sons

1. Madonna and Christ on the cross.

2. More Madonnas & photos of Hennessy & his mother.

3. More similar pictures & photos round the room.

4. A close-up confirms Hennessy's relationship with his mother.

## Fitz does penance for the women in his life.

1. Fitz weeds his mother's garden.

2. Fitz scrubs Penhaligon's carpet after he has brought dog shit in on his shoe.

3. Fitz tells Judith he needs a holiday. His kneeling position betrays his guilty intention - to go away with Penhaligon.

Penhaligon cries for Giggs. Bilborough plays the father-figure and
warns Penhaligon not to associate with Fitz.

Fitz and Penhaligon cry for their loved ones - Fitz for his son Mark in hospital
with a burst appendix, Penhaligon for Fitz after the explosion.

Tina cries in the interrogation room. "I was born to be a dog."

The final use of liquids as symbols in *To Say I Love You* is to do with the prevention their flow. Sean and Tina wrap their flat in black plastic bin liners to prevent the walls being covered in blood, the liquid of life. Mirroring this is a scene where Fitz waits for Judith at the supermarket and helps to load her car with white plastic bags full of shopping, the 'bread of life'. There is the added signifier of 'black bags', evil, and 'white bags', good. In addition to the black for Sean and Tina and white for Fitz and Judith, Giggs brings Tina a white plastic bag, holding a bottle of wine, when he makes his second and fatal call at her flat, a sign that, despite his impure intentions, he is fighting on the side of good. After the murder of Giggs, Sean and Tina then load their black bundle into the car, mirroring yet again. Each time the plastic fails; Sean is covered in blood, Fitz cannot get Judith to come home, Giggs white bag does not protect him as a magic talisman should, but neither can the black plastic conceal his corpse. McGovern uses the finding of a "johnny" in Giggs wallet as a further ironic indication of the failure of plastic, or rubber in this case, to stop flow; the truth will out.

There is less use of the symbolic power of water in the final story, although there is ample evidence of Fitz drinking. It may simply be that in rewriting at a late stage McGovern was unable to include sophisticated imagery and symbolism. It is raining when the police find Tim's body hanging in the wood, and we hear a woman, Mrs Perry who has guided them there, crying. It is still raining when Bilborough and Penhaligon go to tell the parents; Bilborough plans to tell them but is unable, an echo of his sexual impotence, and Penhaligon has to take over the task. Rain falls when Cassidy is taken out of the police station, a symbol of the grief and anger of the mob outside. In this story, it is Bilborough who has recourse to the restoring powers of the bathroom, retreating to the men lavatory after being reprimanded by his boss rather than having the "cup of tea" suggested by him as a magical cure for all ills.

In this story it is tears that seem to have restorative powers. Tim's mother cries when she is given the shoe and again when she appeals for clues to her son's murder on television. It is the sight of her tears which provoke Mrs Perry to go to the police and tell the truth. Tim's mother and brother both cry tears of guilt when Fitz talks to them, the mother expresses her "relief about the murder", Andy feels guilty he did not prevent it. Cassidy also cries when Fitz accuses him of the murder at the hotel. In contrast to these tears of grief

<u>To Say I Love You</u> - Plastic as a barrier to the flow of liquid. ILL.34.

1. Tina cuts the black plastic bin bags.

2. Tina begins her bizarre decorating.

3. Fitz helps Judith load her white shopping bags into her car.

4. Tina strips Sean ready for action.

5. Giggs brings Tina a gift of wine wrapped in white plastic - despite his lewd intentions this signifies that Giggs is a 'good' guy'.

6. Sean & Tina load Giggs corpse, now wrapped in black plastic, into the car.

7. The 'magic' bottles help Fitz find the condom in Giggs belonging which will point the way to his murderers.

are those shed in joy by Bilborough and his wife at the birth of their baby; as one family suffers a loss another has a gain, the circularity of the wheel of life.

There is a strange play of cups and drinks at the police station during the celebration over Bilborough becoming a father. Fitz appears to be drinking a cup of coffee, when a young policeman staggers in laden with cans of beer, followed by Beck carrying two bottles of champagne. Beck then pours champagne into Fitz cup so when he takes a coffee to Cassidy in his cell, Fitz is in fact drinking alcohol. The deception over drinks echoes his intended deception of going on holiday with Penhaligon, Fitz deceiving Judith and Penhaligon deceiving her work mates. The look Beck gives Penhaligon when giving her a drink as she leaves the room suggests he shares Fitz lustful feeling towards her. Fitz problems do not end here, Cassidy telling Fitz that he "wants him to kill again", so Fitz can find out what it is like to be responsible for a death. Fitz had offered "to share the burden" with Cassidy, but gets more than he bargained for, he realises he has made a terrible mistake. The look of recognition on Fitz's face echoes the look of recognition on Cassidy's face when Fitz tells him, at the top of the tower building, that Tim was murdered and did not commit suicide as Cassidy had thought.

1. The corpse in the wood.

2. The search for Tim in the rain.

3. The light illuminates Tim's shoe.

4. Rain adds gloom to Bilborough's sad task.

5. It is raining again during the second search. The torches find the corpse.

6. Rain again when Tim's parents learn of his death.

7. More rain when Cassidy is released from the police station but not from his torment.

1. Tim's mother cries for him, his father can not.

2. Mrs. Perry will be moved by a mother's tears and go to the police.

3. Andy cries guilty tears for his brother Tim.

4. Tim's mother shares her grief with Fitz

5. Cassidy cries at the hotel with Fitz & Beck

6. Bilborough & his wife cry tears of joy for their new baby

1. A policeman brinks beer to celebrate Bilborough becoming a father.

2. Fitz drinks coffee.

3. Beck brings champagne. He has shaved off his moustache. The phallic bottles underline his need to prove his masculinity.

4. Bilborough teases Beck with a false moustache. Bilborough has proved his masculinity by becoming a father.

5. Bilborough's teasing makes Beck 'ejaculate'.

6. Fitz's coffee cup is filled with champagne.

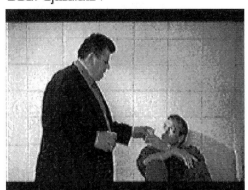

7. Fitz takes Cassidy a coffee. Cassidy shares his burden with Fitz.

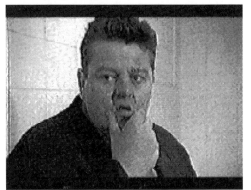

8. Recognition. Fitz realises he has made a mistake.

## HEROES AND REVENGE

"Before setting out on revenge, first dig two graves" [171]

"A man who studies revenge keeps his own wounds green." [172]

Fundamental to Elizabethan and Jacobean tragedy is the belief that clever evil men may outwit themselves and be hoist by their own petard. Thus it is that Revenge may turn on the revenger and bring about his downfall. So it is with Vindici in *The Revenger's Tragedy*, Vindici's vanity in his cleverness at exacting revenge on the Duke and his family causing him to brag of their murders. Similarly, Fitz is caught by his own cleverness when he has an innocent man arrested, harassed, and abandoned by his loved ones in *One Day A Lemming will Fly*. Fitz cleverness is also one of the reason his wife Judith leaves him. She tells him, "The way you probe is boring.; the way you analyse is boring. Your search for the bloody pure motive is boring." [173] So how is it that we remain sympathetic to Fitz and not bored by his search, and how did Jacobean playwrights manage to extract sympathy for their vengeful heroes from the audience ?

London audiences were accustomed to heroes who held revenge as a duty. Whilst there was no universal accepted doctrine of revenge, there was a widely held assumption in Jacobean England that the law barred from inheritance a son who refused to avenge a wrong done to his father. The orthodox Christian position was that God would avenge. Divine vengeance might either be direct and miraculous, through magistrates or through mental agony of the wicked. There was no place for private revenge, indeed English law forbade it, holding it as no more than premeditated murder. This , of course, did not apply to monarchs. The doctrine of Tudor and Stuart monarchs and the Reformed church was that kings could only be punished by God and their subjects should obey even tyrants. Mediaeval theorists supported tyranicide, Sidney, in book II of *Arcadia* calls it "heroic". An older tradition, alive, but not officially accepted, did sanction revenge. Private revenge was allowable for blood kin, motivated by a desire for justice not passion. Although the courts forbade murder as revenge for murder, they

---

[171] Chinese proverb. James Bond to Melina, whose parents have been killed by 'baddies', in For Your Eyes Only, UA (UK) 1981

[172] Sir Francis Bacon. The Hunter in Spiderman, (Live & Kicking, BBC1,TX 10.2.96.)

[173] To Say I Love You, sc.9. p.18

permitted retaliation in kind to victims of 'mayhem'. This can be seen as the Old Testament doctrine of ' an eye for an eye'. The net result was that the English people expected private revenge if the law failed. Furthermore, the instinct to avenge kin-murder was regarded as a manifestation of natural law and the avenger suffered no pangs of conscience. The revenge of passion was another matter, always thoroughly evil. Such revenge stems from man's animal nature, for the passions have psychological causes. Italian doctrine was subtlety different. As stated in Sir William Segar's "The Booke of Honor and Armes"; " for revenge of ... cawardlie and bestiall offences, it is allowable to use any advantages or sublettie."[174] In Italian popular tradition private revenge was permissible when the law did not act, as long as standards were met. The revenger had to destroy both spirit and body of his victim in order for his pride to be assuaged. The more treacherous and cruel Italianate revenges were condemned by the English, who feared their importation. The Italians were reputed to exact a terrible penalty for the slightest injury, to carry on long vendettas and to torture their dying victims in body and soul in order to secure their eternal damnation. It is clear then, why tragic playwrights chose to set their work in Italianate settings. Not only could they avoid the retribution of political criticism, they could allow their characters to behave in an Italian fashion; exacting terrible revenge whilst keeping the sympathy of the audience. So Vindici in *The Revenger's Tragedy* is allowed to revenge the death of his betrothed as no civil justice is possible. We know this since she has died of poison either at the hands of the duke or self-inflicted as a result of her dishonour by him. Man-made justice will allow the execution of Vindici at the end of the play however, when he is condemned by the hand of Antonio despite the fact that his vengeance has also avenged the dishonour and death of Antonio's wife.

Frank Krutnik gives three categories of masculine hero found in film noir. First, in the investigative thriller, there is a hero who is a great professional detective. He seeks to restore order and validate his own identity by exposing and countermanding a criminal conspiracy. Second, in the male suspense thriller, is the hero who finds himself in an inferior position, both to the police and criminals. He must restore his position by eradicating the enigma. Third, in the criminal-adventure thriller, comes the hero, usually aided by a woman, who wilfully or accidentally engages in a crime and has

---

[174] London. 1590.p.20

to face the consequences. [175] In contemporary television terms these translate as the 'gentleman detective', for example, *Sherlock Holmes, Inspector Morse*, etc, the ' unwitting or dodgy detective', for example, *Spender, The Beiderbecke Affair* , and the 'tragic hero', for example Sean in *Cracker - To Say I Love You. Cracker* offers the viewer two types of hero in the noir mould as described. Fitz is in some sense a 'gentleman detective' who, like Sherlock Holmes, operates on the side of the law, but not from within it. Like Sherlock Holmes, Fitz is in search of the truth which sometimes makes him at odds with the police. McGovern describes Fitz as a man "in search of a pure motive," [176] a man willing to probe deeply to find the truth. As I have already mentioned, truth and justice are not always the same thing, and in the rush to see justice done in The Name of the Law, the truth is sometimes obscured. McGovern wanted to create a character who probed deeply to get at the truth, to uncover the motive behind the crime. He says, "I was always a fan of *The Human Jungle* - Herbert Lom. But Herbert Lom used to just say 'this is wrong with you, you set fire to the hamsters at school' and end of programme. There was no in depth probing with Herbert Lom."[177] McGovern wanted a character who really got to the 'why' of the matter and did not just come up with a clever conclusion out of thin air. However, Fitz's constant probing not only makes him unpopular with the regular 'on the beat' detectives it also causes him marital problems. It is obvious that Fitz's cleverness and wit attracted him to Judith. McGovern says that they "mapped out" the fact that Fitz and Judith were students together and "he charmed the pants off her." He says Fitz was, "never the most attractive man in the world, but he had a brain and he knows that." He suggests that Fitz seduced Judith by telling her, "I know what's at the bottom of your heart," but actually told her "what's at the bottom of his heart, but because we're all human beings it all sort of chimes in and she thinks he's accurate but really he's examining himself." [178] Fitz need to probe stems from his need to prove himself and becomes an obsession. He often says he is bored, using this an excuse for his gambling, and eventually Judith finds "your search for that bloody pure motive boring. It's as boring as living with the bloody Pope..." [179] What first attracted her now causes her to leave. Krutnik suggests that noir heroes often demonstrate an obsession with their

---

[175]  In A Lonely Street - Film noir, genre and masculinity. p.86
[176]  Authors interview, 5.2.96.
[177]  Desert Island Discs
[178]  Authors interview, 5.2.96.
[179]  To Say I Love You, sc.9.p.18

impaired or failed masculinity. If we accept that Fitz proves his masculinity by proving his intelligence, as we know he considers this to be the way in which he is attractive to women, we can understand his obsessive need for eternal probing. Coltrane shares this obsession with the character he plays, as many people have reported he constantly shows his intelligence with "fact after fact", "witticisms" and the like. Fitz's need to prove himself is evident because the minute Judith leaves home he turns to Penhaligon for attention  He is very childlike in his need and, like many noir heroes, turns to a dominant or powerful woman for comfort. Penhaligon has to be seen as a powerful woman in this respect because she is independent, unmarried and separate from her own family, she has a 'masculine' job where she can make decisions and take control of situations and she is given access to male icons, for what could be more phallic than a gun. In this way, Fitz's cleverness is both his strength and his weakness. Krutnik suggests two further weaknesses demonstrated by noir heroes, an incapacity to extricate themselves and a readiness to submit to debasement, thus causing their downfall. Fitz is unable to extricate himself from his addiction to gambling, even when it means he could lose his wife forever. He subverts the gamblers anonymous session Judith has insisted he attend by starting a card game. He has to beg forgiveness from Penhaligon for using her as a pawn to try and make Judith and then further debases himself by having to borrow money from her. While this does not diminish her feelings for him it places Fitz in her power when before he had been the dominant one.

*Cracker,* because of its detective genre, allows us the possibility of a second hero in each story. In addition to this, some of the supporting characters also display heroic qualities at times. In the first *Cracker* story we have Kelly, a tragic hero wrongly accused of a crime who has to try to prove his innocence. He is unable to extricate himself without the help of Fitz and is also willing to submit to debasement, even offering to confess to the murder to stop the torment of not knowing. While Kelly seeks to clear his name Fitz fulfils the role of Revenger, seeking to avenge the wrong done to a loved one, his student and symbolic daughter, by catching the murderer. Because the girl is a symbolic daughter to Fitz, he is allowed to be brutal in his investigations, even when questioning the tragic hero, Kelly. This is in the tradition of Jacobean tragedy; a Revenger may seek retribution for blood-kin where the law fails. The Law is seen to have failed by asking Fitz for help, even if on this occasion he offers help before it is acknowledged by the police. In the second story, Sean and Tina are classic tragic hero and heroine, as mentioned before, director Andy Wilson always saw this as the case. Sean is representative of those noir heroes drawn into crime through their association with what Krutnik describes as "phallic" women. Like Neff in *Double Indemnity*, Sean may have turned to crime eventually but it is the femme fatal who is the catalyst. Naturally heroes of this type are made vulnerable by love, which leads to their tragic downfall. In the third story is a hero who seems to be unable to escape his role as victim. Cassidy, as the wrongly accused man, can only pray for "him to kill again" while he is held in prison as a means to prove his innocence. Since he holds himself responsible for the boy's death we only remain sympathetic to Cassidy because he has already suffered retribution.

## MOTHERS & FATHERS

We are not allowed to lose sympathy for Fitz, despite all his problems and weaknesses, because it is necessary to sustain his character throughout the series. I have mentioned that this is partly because he is both Father and Child still fighting the Oedipal dilemma. If families are absent in noir, nevertheless, a father-figure is often killed, like Keyes and Dietrichson in *Double Indemnity* or Nick in *The Postman Always Rings Twice* In *Cracker* Bilborough, who has a strange father-son, son-father relationship with Fitz, eventually dies. By this time Bilborough's character has been developed to make him a real father, but McGovern sacrifices him like a Christ figure. Family conflict in *Cracker* often seems to stem from a reaction against the patriarchal order; Tina's father is stern and intractable just as Fitz's father in law is. Mother figures are very important in *Cracker*, while the absence of a loving mother leads to crime, for example Tina's mother could have compensated for the sternness of her husband, too great a mother-love can also lead to problems. The murderer in *The Mad Woman In The Attic* turns to crime on the death of his mother, the dominance of female influence leads to Tim's death in "One Day A Lemming Will Fly". Winterbottom fore - grounded the importance of Hennessy's mother by asking Designer Chris Wilkinson to place several images of mother and child in his house. There are pictures of the Madonna all over the house as well as photographs of Hennessy with his mother. Although Hennessy obviously has a weak father, these images emphasise his Oedipal problems and point the way for Fitz to suspect him as the murderer. In fact it as if Hennessey's mother 'tells' or 'points the way' to Fitz as the most clear and obvious photograph of Hennessey with his mother comes directly before Fitz asks if he can use the bathroom, certainly the maternal force working for good and truth.

Fitz also loves his mother dearly, in fact McGovern says he "worshipped the ground she walked on."[180] Fitz problem with his mother is guilt. McGovern says Fitz feels responsible for her and feels guilty when he does not go to see her, but "the less often he goes the harder it is to go". [181] Then, of course, he feels more guilty because he has not been to see her, a viscous circle of Catholicism. McGovern based much of Fitz mother, played by Beryl Reid, on his own mother, of whom he is very fond. Fitz picking out horses with his mother is purely biographical says McGovern, who still takes his mother to Bingo on a Wednesday night. Fitz and his mother have a loving and natural relationship, she has never lost sympathy for him as he is still her little boy. The portrayal of their relationship represents the only real stability in Fitz's life and is a big clue to why he remains sympathetic to the viewer. In a later series we do find out that Fitz resented his father for taking away his mother and harboured murderous feelings towards him. The fact that he overcame these feelings is another indication that. despite all his other faults, Fitz is a stable character who will survive. Fitz can thus fulfil the function of noir hero, but he can never be a truly tragic hero and in this he differs from the Revengers of the Jacobean tradition. Perhaps in this respect *Cracker* owes more to its noir roots than to its Jacobean ones, a confirmation that while Neal may have created *Cracker*, Fitz is entirely a product of McGovern.

---

[180] Authors interview, 5.2.96.
[181] Ibid.

# CONCLUSION

As I have shown in the evidence given, *Cracker* is a complex drama of the nineties which pays tribute to its diverse literary, dramatic and visual roots.

Its structure as a dramatic tragedy would appear to come mostly from a tradition of Jacobean drama, and therefore through the influence of Gub Neal, its producer. Its narrative, both story and visual interpretation, however would seem to have strong elements of film noir: The types of heroes, both detective and tragic, the use of expressionistic composition, the symbolic use of light and dark and water, and the characteristic urban setting, suggest the theme and mood of *Cracker* is mainly influenced by its author, Jimmy McGovern, and the treatment of his writing by directors, designer and cinematographer.

This dualism might seem at first to be a problem, but through investigation I have proved that many elements of film noir share the same roots as Jacobean tragedy. The English tragedy which came to us from the Greeks, passing through Elizabethan and Jacobean drama, developed through the classic nineteenth century novel and the 'gentleman' detective before taking the various forms of drama on television today. The American drama from which film noir springs also comes from the Greek tradition, developing through pulp detective fiction with its less refined, more hard-bitten heroes.

It is important to remember the influence of émigrés from Europe on the development of film noir which account for much of its visual style and to bear in mind the fact that these influences continued in Europe and still influence film production today. One must also not forget that D.W.Griffiths, the father of American film, was steeped in literary tradition and the sensibilities of Dickens, Tolstoy, Frank Norris and Walt Whitman display themselves in his work. Just as Europe influenced America, now America influences Europe, so it should be no surprise that so much of today's television references genres which have become part of our shared cultural inheritance.

*Cracker* is a success because it is constructed in such a way as to make available a wealth of referents and present them to its audience in a form which can be appreciated on a number of levels. Thus the audience is stimulated visually, emotionally, intellectually and culturally. Much of this is achieved on a sub-conscious, or subliminal, level only obvious through the kind of careful and detailed study of the text I have made. By the use of archetypes and narrative techniques developed over centuries, *Cracker* is able to present to-day's dilemmas in a cultural form comfortable to its audience. Just as Griffiths borrowed from nineteenth century literature to forge the new art of the twentieth century - cinema, so too Cracker draws on established literary and cinematic traditions to forge a new vision for television into the next century. *Cracker* is the natural culmination of a cultural inheritance we share with Europe and America, and as such was crafted to turn tragedy into success.

## CRITICAL RESPONSE

When critics previewed *Cracker* as "blackly entertaining" [182] , "dynamic drama" [183] , "brilliant but wild", "gritty",[184] "a cracker of a programme", "gripping and stylish", "impressive", [185] "tense drama",[186] "glossy, £3 million production", [187] "better than *Prime Suspect*" [188] it was obvious audiences were in for a treat. *Cracker* certainly lived up to the fanfare of publicity which preceded its release. Both critics and viewers were delighted with its originality, energy and style, although some critics took some persuading at first. Matthew Norman found the script "sharp throughout" , "the atmospherics and pace nicely judged" and predicted the series " ought to dominate the awards ceremonies and the ratings for a very long time to come." [189] Thomas Sutcliffe found the plot "solidly constructed, offering you a whole range of pleasures", "a sense of lives extending beyond the frame of the story", details "great" and the camerawork "restive" and "ingenious".[190] Compton Miller thought "Coltrane's Cracker takes the biscuit" and after an hour had "come round to Coltrane's surprise casting," [191] unlike Peter Barnard who, with the headline "Comic turns to crime", found it difficult to resolve the "identity problem" caused by the "attempt to tell two stories at once." [192] Peter Paterson also began watching with "a certain amount of wariness and suspicion" but soon discovered "an original and highly entertaining thriller" in which the "dangerous ploy" of offering us "two parallel but apparently unconnected stories" was justified when they started to converge. This combined with "taut writing, plenty of tension, some wry

---

[182]   Tina Ogle - Time Out, 22.9.93.

[183]   Yorkshire Evening Press, 27.9.93.

[184]   Graham Keal - Northern Echo, 23.9.93.

[185]   Hello, 25.9.93.

[186]   TV Times, 25.9.93.

[187]   Rob Driscoll - Birmingham Evening Post, 25.9.93.

[188]   Peter Grant - Liverpool Echo, 27.9.93.

[189]   London Evening Standard, 28.3.93.

[190]   The Independent, 28.9.93.

[191]   Daily Express, 28.9.93.

[192]   The Times, 28.9.93.

humour and sharp characterisation" made *Cracker* "highly watchable". [193]
Gary Leboff described *Cracker* as "enthralling, if macabre, twist to
crimebusting drama" and loved Coltrane as a "superb...brooding figure." [194]
"Powerful, tense and extremely watchable," was how Simon London
described *Cracker*, although John Gibson could not understand it at all and
asked "what's all the hype about ?"[195]  Pam Francis could not "wait to see
how Fitz catches out the man with no memory" even though she was
troubled by "disturbing material" shown "where this poor girl had been
butchered like an abattoir."[196] The New Statesman's critic also could not
"bear to wait another week for episode two," but had no problem with the
sex and violence. S/He found the writing, "complemented by Michael
Winterbottom's superb direction" "intense and gripping," "at one moment
terrifying, another hilarious, and the forensic expert "specially impressive" as
he asked "Can you just get one of me pointing at it ... something for the
album ?"[197] "Coltrane's cracked it" headlined Margaret Forwood's column
and she demanded that her readers should watch "the most successful
debut of the season" as "Monday nights with Cracker have instantly
become a must." [198]

The Press continued to praise the series as "gripping mystery", "special",
"an ingenious, atmospheric thriller", and to headline reviews with "It's a
cracker !", "Cracker of a role", "Cracker Coltrane" . Before the second
episode was transmitted on 4th. October 1993, the News Of The World had
already deemed *Cracker* a "great psychological thriller," [199] and the
Liverpool Echo tipped the series for viewing as "Jim's best work to date." [200]
This "powerful new detective drama with a difference" was Tonight's choice
in the Eastern Evening News, [201] Critics choice in  The Sunday Times, [202]

[193]  TV Mail Reviews, 28.9.93.
[194]  The Sun, 28.9.93.
[195]  Edinburgh Evening News, 28.9.93.
[196] Today, 28.9.93.
[197]  New Statesman, 1.10.93.
[198]  Daily Express, 2.10.93.
[199]  The News Of The World, 3.10.93.
[200]  Liverpool Echo, 4.10.93.
[201]  4.10.93.

and recommended in Telegraph's Today's highlights.[203]  The Northern Echo promised that *Cracker* would grip your attention " to the finish"[204]  and the Sun  warning advice, "Don't miss this".[205] By the following morning John Ogden's headline read "Coltrane's the perfect choice" [206] and Pam Francis was "crackers  about Cracker. " [207] Maureen Paton thought "Granada's witty psychological thriller Cracker maintained its moody Chanderesque style" [208] and Simon London found *Cracker* "still made gripping television" [209] . Pat Moore advised "you either accept Fitz ... from the start or switch off for the next five episodes" and praised it as "punchily written... and pacily directed." [210]  Journalists could not wait to write articles with titles like "Big Hero", [211] "Big Shrink", [212] " Robbie Fitz the Bill", [213] "Robbie's quit drink to shrink",[214] "Fitz adds a drop of fizz",[215] "Fitz of frustration".[216]

There was no doubt in the critics minds that this new series had quality and style, and viewing figures showed that audiences agreed.  The Liverpool Echo reported *Cracker* had "regularly pulled in more than 11 million viewers",[217]  the Daily Post noted that it was "topping the popularity charts",[218] the Financial Times reported the "rapid success" of the series.[219] Gary Leboff awarded *Cracker* "the autumn honours",[220] and Simon London promised to make his own award if Cracker "misses out when the BAFTA

---

[202]  3.10.93.

[203]  Richard Bruton, 4.10.93.

[204]  4.10.93.

[205]  Sun TV, 4.10.93.

[206]  Wolverhampton Express & Star, 5.10.93.

[207]  Today, 5.10.93.

[208]  Daily Express, 5.10.93.

[209]  Daily Mirror, 5.10.93.

[210]  The Stage and Television Today, 7.10.93.

[211]  Anne Pickles - Yorkshire Evening Post, 8.10.93.

[212]  Graham Young -  Telly Mail, 9.10.93.

[213]  Lucy Broadbent - Today  TV week, 25.9.93. to 1.10.93.

[214]  Fiona Knight

[215]  Richard Middleton - Daily Star, 11.10.93.

[216]  Shropshire Star, 16.10.93.

[217]  Peter Grant, 8.11.93.

[218]  8.11.93.

[219]  Christopher Dunkley, 8.11.93.

[220]  The Sun, 9.11.93.

awards come round".[221] Everyone predicted that *Cracker* would be back "by popular request" [222] and Elizabeth Cowley, perhaps with an inside source, was confident enough to say that "a new series of Cracker has been confirmed" [223]

From referring back to the viewing figures compiled by BARB (see Fig. 1), it is easy to see how the audience increased over the first series and how Granada could expect a substantial audience for subsequent series. In fact *Cracker* managed to maintain larger audiences for series two and three by attracting new viewers in addition to keeping loyal original viewers.

In 1993 the Royal Television Society Programme and Technology Awards voted *Cracker* as Best Drama Series, confirming its acceptance within the industry, and Robbie Coltrane was presented with the award for Best Male Performer, his first recognition as a 'serious' actor. The TV Quick Awards confirmed *Cracker's* popularity with audiences when it received the award for Best Newcomer (Drama Programme), also in 1993. Jimmy McGovern also received the vote of the people when he was awarded the Whitbread Scousology Award - TV Personality in 1994. Audiences continued to be loyal to the series, and by 1995 voted Cracker the LLoyds Bank Peoples Choice award for Most Popular Drama Series at the BAFTA Awards that year. Sadly, and despite many nominations, the first series of Cracker only received two BAFTA Awards in 1994, Best Actor going to Robbie Coltrane and Ivan Strasberg receiving the award for Best Film / TV Photography (Fiction). It deserved more, and was more successful at other awards ceremonies. The 1994 Broadcasting Press Guild Awards for Best Series went to Robbie Coltrane - Best Actor and Jimmy McGovern - Best Writer. McGovern also won the Writers Guild Award. Technical and artistic excellence was recognised with Royal Television Society, Commercial & Design Awards going to Oral Norey Ottey for editing *To Say I Love You*, Helen King for make-up on series one, and to the sound team, Phil Smith

---

[221] TV Daily Mirror, 9.11.93.
[222] Richard Bruton - Telegraph , 8.11.93.
[223] Daily Mail, 8.11.93.

and Tony Cooper, for *The Mad Woman In The Attic.* Europe also recognised Cracker's worth with Robbie Coltrane winning the Silver Nymph Award for Outstanding Performance at the Television Festival of Monte Carlo and being nominated in the top ten list of International Quality TV Programmes at The Cologne conference in 1994. the 1995 FIPA TV Awards in Nice brought Coltrane another Best Actor award. Robbie Coltrane again won Best Actor at the 1995 BAFTA Awards where *Cracker* was at last voted Best Drama Series, and Jimmy McGovern was visibility moved when he accepted the newly created Dennis Potter Award for his outstanding writing. By this time sales in America had prompted the awards of Best Movie or Miniseries, Best Actor in a Movie or Miniseries - Robbie Coltrane and Best Director of a Movie or Miniseries to Andy Wilson, all for *To Say I Love You.* The Mystery Writers of America awarded the Edgar Allan Poe Award to Jimmy McGovern for the script of *To Say I Love You.* Unable to fly the Atlantic Jimmy graciously accepted the award, invariably won by British crime writers, by telephone and waited for it to be delivered by post. I hope he will forgive me for repeating the "funny story" he told me about it. Having won by now several prestigious awards and received a variety of statuettes McGovern naturally expected similar from the USA, particularly after his win had been announced by fax describing the grand ceremony, five star hotel on the West Coast and the "fine porcelain figure" which would be "double wrapped and double wrapped and double wrapped and insured and we just hope it reaches you in one piece." The Edgar Allan Poe Award duly arrived. Having asked if I remembered the old fairgrounds where you threw three darts at a card, Jimmy told me "well this (the award) is what you got, its the cheapest shoddy piece of shit you've ever seen in your life. Its blue, black and white and Edgar Allan Poe's got this big droopy moustache and it looks diabolical." Well, I suppose it's the thought that counts, isn't it?

FIG. 2

## Viewing figures for *Cracker* - series one given by BARB are:

*The Mad Woman In The Attic* -    episode 1: TVR - 19.1 %
                                               audience - 10.084 million
                                               audience share -45.6%
                                  episode 2: TVR - 18.9 %
                                               audience - 9.987 million
                                               audience share - 44.8%


*To Say I Love You-*              episode 3: TVR - 18.6 %
                                               audience - 9.831 million
                                               audience share - 44.8%
                                  episode 4: TVR - 18.7 %
                                               audience - 9.883 million
                                               audience share -43.4%
                                  episode 5:  TVR - 20.3 %
                                               audience - 10.713 million
                                               audience share - 45 %


*One Day A Lemming will Fly* -    episode 6: TVR - 22.6 %
                                               audience - 11.942 million
                                               audience share - 50.1 %
                                  episode 7: TVR - 22.6 %
                                               audience - 11.935 million
                                               audience share - 50.6 %


The average figures during series one from 27.9.93. to 8.11.93. -
            over seven transmissions was : TVR - 20.1 %
                                               audience 10.616 million
                                               audience share - 46.2.%


Series two - from 10.10.94. to 5.12.94. -
            average over nine transmissions : TVR - 24.5 %
                                               audience - 13.45 million
                                               audience share - 51.8 %


Series three -transmitted 16.10.95. to 27.11.95
            average over eight transmissions : TVR - 26.3 %
                                               audience - 13.986 million
                                               audience share -51.8%[224]

---

[224] TVR - Target viewers reached
      audience - total viewers
      audience share - share of audience compared to other channels

# THE TEAM

## THE EXECUTIVE PRODUCER

Some time in 1992, with the end of Inspector Morse heralded, **Sally Head,** Controller of Drama at Granada Television, began to look around for a new detective series to fill the slot.  So did other heads of drama. Matthew Norman described how "frantic executives throughout the network ... desperately searched  for a replacement, a new crime solver to be their home banker in terms of both critical appreciation and ratings." [225] Head knew she needed something different if she was to capture a prime time slot once again, and repeat the success she had had with *Prime Suspect.*

## THE PRODUCER

Producer **Gub Neal**, prompted by the success of *Silence Of The Lambs,* came up with an idea for a crime series which was a 'why dunnit " rather than a 'who dunnit'. Jimmy McGovern told The Independent, "Everybody wanted to do a series on a criminal psychologist because *Silence Of The Lambs* had been a huge hit." Everyone including, apparently,  fellow Liverpudlian Lynda La Plante had ideas along those lines. But, says Jimmy proprietarily, "Fitz is mine." [226]  Neal felt the time was right for psychology to take over from the 'bang them to rights' approach of 'cops and robbers' police series and the Victorian style guesswork of gentleman detectives. Many agreed with him including Thomas Sutcliffe wrote, "After a decade of judicial miscarriages, it's hardly surprising that the whodunnit should have given way to the didhedoit (the same device that gave the first *Prime Suspect* its real charge)." [227] Neal also realised the importance of bringing something different  to a new series. He wanted a series which would

---

[225]  The London Evening Standard, 28.9.93.

[226]  Independent On Sunday, 5.2.95.

appeal to "us", that is to say people with an education, a diverse set of influences, without losing the qualities which would make it reach the greatest popular audience. Neal and his script editors, Catriona McKenzie and Nicola Shindler, felt that storytelling in television did not have to be any more mundane than it already was. Neal says, "television can either be completely banal and deal with the everyday and represent a kind of moral affirmation of expectations, values and so on, and to some extent that's what *Lovejoy, Pie In The Sky, Morse* and essentially generic television serials represent, or it can aim a bit higher by trying to create something which is a bit more diverse and in a sense more complex, though not necessarily more complicated, in its range and also in terms of how it appeals to people." [228] He was determined to aim 'a bit higher' and succeeded. As director Simon Cellan Jones says, "*Cracker* combines many things, like being socially relevant. It was a great hit among the chattering classes, it was lovely for them to be able to intellectualise as well as simply watch. One of the benchmarks of a television success is people chattering about it afterwards."[229]

Neal knew that any new series would require a central figure for audiences to identify with and around whom the series could be built and then marketed. He wanted a character who was "fundamentally dangerous and unpredictable and at the same time embodied a certain heroic quality" which you could "admire and respect". [230] Neal was confident that he could get support for such a character from Sally Head ,who is well known for her love of 'dangerous combinations' and her ability bring together volatile elements and shape them into strong products.

[227]  The Independent, 28.9.93.

[228]  Authors interview,  20.4.94.

[229]  Authors interview,  30.11.95.

[230]  Ibid.

# THE WRITER

"If you haven't got the story, you haven't got anything."[231]

It was vital to find a writer possessed of unique insights and abilities in order to bring such a character to life, someone who "subverts the genre and subverts the normal in terms of expectations." [232]  Neal told The Yorkshire Evening Press," What was critical for me was to find a writer prepared to jump into investigative drama and a lead character unlike any of the other detective characters around."[233]  So, with a clear idea for a series which would have strong plot lines but be motivated by this disruptive character, Neal approached Liverpool writer **Jimmy McGovern** to write a draft script. Neal knew that McGovern, with eighty episodes of *Brookside* to his credit and with his recent win of The Samuel Beckett Award for his screenplay Needle, could write equally well for maximum popular audiences and for more exploratory territory reached on BBC2. McGovern already had a reputation for controversy, the writer responsible for the rape of Sheila Grant in *Brookside*, in Needle he dealt with a city in the grip of a drugs crisis. McGovern would deny that he is controversial although he does like to stir up "massive, massive debates."[234] He says, "I do like getting a bloody good story wrapped around a bloody good theme." [235]  McGovern sees no difference in audience needs and expectation either. "I write," he says modestly, " I tell the story." [236] Although he has dealt with issues as provoking as rape, racism, drug abuse and  homosexuality, at the heart of his stories there is often a love story. If you want to know what sort of man McGovern is you only have to look at his choice of record and luxury on his recent broadcast of *Desert Islands Discs*. McGovern the romantic chooses *When I Fall in Love* sung by Nat King Cole , "for my Mam, who used to sing

---

[231]  Attributed to Raoul Walsh by Martin Scorsese, A Personal Journey With Martin Scorsese Through American Movies, BFI, C4, (21.5.95)

[232]  Ibid.

[233]  27.9.93.

[234]  Independent On Sunday, 5.2.95.

[235]  Daily Telegraph, 2.2.95.

[236]  Authors interview, 5.2.96.

it going round the house, a little two up, two down, loads of kids, it's stuck with me ever since."[237] but the realist in him asks for haemorrhoid ointment as a luxury because ," I had to pick a thing that I always take along with me no matter where I go, and the thing I always take along with me is haemorrhoid ointment so it would have to be that." "Raw to the end," comments Sue Lawley with an unknowing pun. [238] *Needle* was the love story of a young couple forced into marriage by teenage pregnancy, drug abuse merely a symptom of the hero's struggle to survive in "post-ideology Britain".[239] The central theme of *To Say I Love You* is not the murder of loan shark Cormack and policeman Giggs,  but the desperate love Sean and Tina have for one another. [240] *Priest* too is a love story, although there is no denying the controversy of the love of a Catholic priest for another man. Life somehow has a knack of getting in the way of love, and therein lies the tragedy.

 McGovern was an ideal choice for a producer who needed tough characters and gutsy writing and Neal's own outline provided an excellent structure in which to set the series. Each acknowledges the work of the other man. "Jimmy was able to hothouse the ideas for *Cracker* with two or three other people," says Neal," but Jimmy animated it and brought it to life and did all the things that make it work."[241]  McGovern says," The story brings a structure of its own then, only then, do you sit down and examine the structure. I worry about the structure after. I find people who go on at enormous length about structure do because there's nothing in the content. I do structure,  but what happens is the first draught is shown to so many people and its they who adhere to those rules. For instance in *To Say I Love You* I got an enormous number of notes to the effect we've got to understand Sean and Tina, got to know who they are. Of course I did as I was told and wrote some nice scenes between Sean and Tina early on,

[237]  Desert Island Discs, BBC Radio 4, TX: 14.1.96. RPT: 19.1.96.
[238]  Ibid
[239]  Jimmy McGovern, Independent On Sunday, 5.2.95.
[240]  Cracker, series 1,eps. 3,4,5.
[241]  Authors interview, 20.4.94.

holding up the plot and sure enough in the edit those are the ones that go because the script's too long."[242] McGovern recognised the continuing hard work of producer, directors and script editors who, along with himself, would "sit there until two or three in the morning" at what he vividly describes as "the night of the long knives" every night after a script read- through." We would realise the script was drastically over so every single story has this night of the long knives. It got really painful, the stuff we had to cut. And you'd see the actors who'd been to the read-through, they were just about to get pissed and go shagging each other and we were all working ." "Surely not" , I protested at this point. " "They're all tarts," continued Jimmy, "as you well know. We were just knackered. Even then we were cutting when we got into the edit suite.[243] Praise where praise is due and biting honesty, another thing McGovern is renowned for and proud of. Talking about *Cracker* to Sue Lawley, McGovern says," I suspect he's fairly honest, Fitz. I think he says an awful lot of things I know an awful lot of men feel uncomfortable with, but I think he speaks the truth." and when questioned about writing about dark issues in the series he replies," in *Cracker* there are huge issues there - racism and rape in the same programme, that's huge to tackle. I think I approached that with honesty and integrity, its dangerous stuff but it's not there because I want to shock people."[244] .

## THE LEADING MAN

Having established McGovern as complementary to the more formal talents of himself and his script editors [245] Neal needed to find an actor capable of carrying the strong central role. Before McGovern had agreed to write what

---

[242] Authors interview, 5.2.96.

[243] Ibid.

[244] Desert Island Discs, BBC Radio 4, TX:14.1.96. RPT: 19.1.96.

[245] Neal graduated from Exeter University with a B.A. in English & American Literature & Commonwealth Studies and later studied at the University of California, Berkeley, USA. Catriona McKenzie graduated in History at Oxford University and Nicola Schindler is an English graduate from Cambridge University.

would become *Cracker,* Neal had approached Robert Lindsay to play the part he envisaged. Lindsay declined saying he did not want to play another hysterical character so soon after "GBH" in case he got typecast. [246] McGovern says, "We didn't have anyone in mind and spent a lot of time thinking "Who are we going to find in their forties who has this amount of danger in them?' " [247] He imagined a thin, wiry guy when he was writing Fitz. "A bit like you ?", Lawley asks McGovern, but he evades a direct answer with, "I used to be thinner and more wiry than this." [248] He had offered an outline to **Robbie Coltrane** who found it "interesting" but wanted to see a script. McGovern was horrified, he saw a John Cassavetes type playing the part. At their first meeting McGovern got completely pissed and told Coltrane to his face that he had seen, and written, Fitz as "a thin man". [249] Later McGovern found Coltrane "had a brilliant mind" and worried that he had offended him.[250] He described his feelings to Lawley, "I was suicidal. I was going to walk. I was on the phone to my agent and then the first few rushes came through and he was absolutely astounding. He lost weight for the part early on, he lost weight and he looked sharp. He was sharp, his brain is so quick. He was perfect."[251]

A man with a history of raising one glass too many, Coltrane did not take offence and admits that he "used to be a bit like that, a bit of a 'boy' "[252] He is referring to Fitz but might well be talking about McGovern, leaving size apart the three have much in common. Neal, talking about his choice of Coltrane for the part, could equally well be describing Fitz when he says, "he has the ability to embrace something that is on the one hand challenging, dangerous, provocative and at the same time there is something quite patriarchal about him. People see someone who has a certain security which we all aspire to and that isn't because he is secure, it's because he

---

[246] "GBH" written by Liverpool writer Alan Bleasdale. Lindsay won a BAFTA as Best Actor for his role in this C4 series.

[247] Time Out, 22.9.93.

[248] Desert Island Discs

[249] Ibid.

[250] Authors interview, April 94.

[251] Desert Island Discs

offers security. It's paternal."[253] This is one of the reasons for the "surprise" casting of Coltrane, his ability to be both outrageous and authoritative at the same time. His 'father figure' makes him attractive to audiences and to Penhaligon alike yet Fitz's (and Coltrane's ?) childishness and inability to cope with his own problems also allows audiences to identify with the child in themselves and to feel sympathy for the character despite his dreadful behaviour. McGovern explains," We all see something inside ourselves that we don't like, and because none of us is unique, the chances are that another person will have shared that experience. You then hit him or her with that and if you hit the target the impact can be devastating. I tend to do myself when I'm pissed and I usually end up getting punched for it."[254] A sound reason to choose Coltrane as an aggressive hero; who would think of punching him. Well, lots might think about it, but most, most <u>men</u> anyway, would never actually do it. In Graham Keal's words "you have to forgive him ... because he's so much bigger than you." [255] The same goes for Fitz. Women get their revenge by other means; Judith by taking away Fitz's most treasured possession, his daughter, Penhaligon more openly by pouring iced water over his head in a restaurant. Neal remembers Coltrane "getting away with it" at their first meeting at the Donmar Warehouse, as recounted in the introduction. There is a sense of both trepidation and admiration for Coltrane in Neal's words. You know at once that this ambitious young man would never drink to excess in the was he has just described, would never behave in a politically incorrect way but somewhere, deep down, is a feeling that he might enjoy the feeling of "getting away with it" if he did. McGovern also recognised the danger embodied in Coltrane telling Tina Ogle," There's a dangerous man within Robbie which he controls now , but you can still feel it."[256] Critics too would find this quality in Coltrane's performance in *Cracker* where "a sense of barely coiled danger"

---

252    Northern Echo, 23.9.93.
253    Authors interview, 20.4.94.
254    Time Out, 22.9.93.
255    Northern Echo, 27.9.93.
256    Time Out, 22.9.93.

was married to "the power to express any emotion". [257] Neal recognised Coltrane's power to hold an audience at once and make no mistake, Coltrane is "on" in front of any audience paying or otherwise. Few people are privileged to see the alter-ego of Robin MacMillan which lies deep beneath the constant performance of Coltrane. "Robbie offers the sense of someone who even if you didn't like them, you wanted to like them." He adds," You'd rather have him as a friend than as an enemy, like the big boy at school, if you're not his friend, you are subject to his abuse."[258] A deep, if unintentional, insight into both men. It is this memory of Coltrane which Neal held in reserve until he needed it, slotting Coltrane neatly into typecast as "the brilliant but wild psychologist Eddie Fitzgerald ... a smoking, drinking gambler with all the manners of a rampaging rhinoceros ."[259] I am not aware of any addiction to gambling but can personally attest to Coltrane's consumption of tobacco and alcohol as well a fondness for Dim Sum and all kinds of good food. Coltrane once described a local cake shop as "temptation with a glass front,"[260] but proved he could combat his over-indulgence by losing several stones in weight to play the part of Fitz. His diet attracted much attention as he declared , "I've made up my mind to lose 10 stone and I'm determined to do it. Alcohol is off, curries are out," [261] "I'm certainly not drinking as much, and I've cut out fat and sugar and curries. Which means I can't eat out in Scotland " [262] and prompted headlines like "Shrink fits the bill as funny man decides to go straight,"[263] "Strong solution in a shrunken shrink", [264] "Coltrane the shrink - Psychologist Robbie sheds six stone to get inside the mind of a murderer." [265] Coltrane was as serious about his diet as he was about conducting research into the role of Fitz. His dedication led him to meet Ian Stephens, one of the leading clinical

---

[257] Matthew Norman - The London Evening Standard, 28.9.93.

[258] Ibid.

[259] Northern Echo, 23.9.93.

[260] Whilst living in Southborough Road, Hackney in the mid-eighties, Coltrane regularly shopped locally in Lauriston Road – now called by 'hipsters' Victoria Park Village.

[261] Shropshire Star, 25.9.93.

[262] Yorkshire on Sunday, 26.9.93.

[263] Phil Penfold- Yorkshire on Sunday, 26.9.93.

[264] Matthew Norman - The London Evening Standard, 28.9.93.

[265] Shropshire Star, 25.9.93.

psychologists in Britain at the State Hospital in Carstairs, the Scottish equivalent of Broadmoor, and to read whatever books he could find on criminal psychology. Even so, he could still joke about both, saying, "When we met we were very civilised, drinking our Diet Cokes while talking about murder."[266] The birth of his son, Spencer, provided an additional incentive. Coltrane says, "It's the baby, I started thinking about when he's five years old and wants to run around the garden. I don't want to be sitting indoors like some wheezy old beggar saying, 'You just run away with your wee friends, son, I'll waddle over later'."[267]

Despite becoming a family man Coltrane has not lost the element of danger which first attracted Neal's attention. He admits to having "a couple of days holiday from my self-imposed diet when we finished making Cracker," and continues," In fact, I happen to know that the end of filming party at a Manchester hotel prompted a complaint from a fellow guest, actress Helen Mirren."[268] Possibly the same party described by Jimmy McGovern ,"There was one night when, at a Cracker wrap party he (Coltrane) had us all in stitches, he was absolutely brilliant. And then at the end of the night he played the piano brilliantly too. And I hated him. I can never be like that."[269] Coltrane was taught to play the piano at an early age, having a musically talented mother. She often used to invite "rather bohemian friends" to the house and give impromptu concerts in the afternoon. Coltrane remembers sitting under the piano whilst very young, soaking in the atmosphere, and puts his love of art and music down to the "artists, Poets, musicians and so on" who used to visit and contribute to his mother's soirees.[270] There is admiration as well as envy for "people like that". McGovern goes on to explain how he envies Coltrane's easy wit, "All those witticisms (in Cracker) take me hours and hours and hours to dream up ... It takes me an awful

[266]   Birmingham Post, 25.9.93.
[267]   Daily Record, 11.10.93.
[268]   Yorkshire on Sunday, 26.9.93.
[269]   Desert Island Discs
[270]   Authors conversations - 1985/6

long time to dream them up." [271] It does not occur to McGovern that Coltrane's 'performance' may take just as much hard work because he makes it look so easy. For Jimmy, just standing up and talking to people takes a supreme effort. He describes at length how he became a wordsmith by having to "pick this work, pick that word," whatever he could get out rather than the most apt word. Sue Lawley asked how he managed his stammer, which was so severe as a child that even his mother needed his elder brother Joey to interpret. McGovern tells her, "by being careful. I'm switching words, using ones I can get out... Even as a child I had loads of words at my disposal. My vocabulary was wide because I was constantly picking words." He became a writer at an early age too because," when I came to write I could pick the mot juste if that's the word, the apt word," and describes his worst nightmare as ,"the school teacher asking me to read my essay, which had all the words in it which were just right but I could never say."[272] You know then why McGovern needs someone to speak his words, get his message across, and why he is so meticulous about his writing. Strange then that he does not see any weakness in Coltrane or acknowledge that his addiction to food and drink is as great as McGovern's own addiction to drink and gambling in the past. They are all compensations for what McGovern calls "a creative void". McGovern stopped gambling to excess when he became a student teacher in the mid-seventies and got "a job where you can exercise your judgement and get the kudos if you're right."[273] Essentially he believes that if you do not use your capacity to think in doing a worthwhile job then you need to expend your energy elsewhere to compensate. It was because he "had things to offer" and "boring mundane jobs" which provided no outlet that he turned to gambling to get a "buzz". McGovern believes that people are afraid of being ordinary and this may be the key to Coltrane's behaviour. In an interview with Graham Keal Coltrane offered this insight into Fitz, "He doesn't cope with his own feelings very well because - like a lot of people - he's got an absolute terror of being

---

[271] Ibid.

[272] Desert Island Discs & conversation with author

[273] Desert Island Discs

ordinary."[274] One might ask 'like Coltrane ?', for while no one would suggest for a moment that Coltrane is ordinary it may be that he has worked hard to make sure that they can not. Many people comment on Coltrane's knowledge and acknowledge that he is passionate about art, politics, film and American cars to name but a few. McGovern describes his "really impressive encyclopaedic knowledge " but found "a stubborn refusal to go deeply into anything." "Most of the time," writes McGovern, "he 'throws floats onto the surface'. That's my analogy for Robbie's conversation which consists of fact after fact." [275]   Could it be that inside this "dangerous" man hides a small boy frightened of being thought ordinary ? With a mother talented in the arts and a strict police surgeon father is it possible that Coltrane, despite being acknowledged as extraordinary by his friends and peers, is still compensating for feelings of inadequacy ? Why is it that Coltrane is recognised by critics as an accomplished actor and yet pronounces the title with self-mocking irony; "Act-or" [276] By choosing to take a degree in fine art at Glasgow School Art and then join the entertainment profession, has Coltrane tried to be as like his mother as possible, or as unlike his father as possible ? Whatever the reasons, Coltrane has certainly demonstrated an understanding of Fitz which deserved the awards he received for his performance. Perhaps it is, that for the first time, Coltrane has been able to channel his intelligence instead covering it under a facade of jokes and wisecracks. And despite all the talent combined in McGovern and Coltrane perhaps none of this would have emerged without the astute Neal to give it air. For although Neal said, "By any stretch of the imagination, the two of them are a risky combination," and journalists called Granada the "biggest gamblers of all," [277] both he and his backers were confident enough to go ahead . Coltrane soon signed a contract, saying, "I wouldn't have done it if it was just another police series. I get offered a lot of TV series and I usually try to avoid them, but this was different." [278] McGovern and Coltrane

---

[274]   Daily Post, 1.10.93.

[275]   Letter,1994

[276]   Peter Barnard - The Times, 28.9.93.

[277]   Northern Echo, 23.9.93.

[278]   Shropshire Star, 25.9.93.

soon began collaborating and the second Cracker story *To Say I Love You* was written with Coltrane specifically in mind. Neal could soon assert that the combination "works brilliantly." [279]

## THE DIRECTORS

"To direct a picture, a man needs humility. Do you have humility Mr......?" [280]

Having captured a writer and a leading man of high calibre, Neal was now faced with the task of hiring directors who would realise the script in sympathy to his own expectations. He wanted to make a popular drama, saying, "In the end , all I'm interested in is popular drama." [281] but it is important to remember that Neal does not consider 'popular' and 'quality' unlikely bedfellows, believing that drama can, and should, be both. He gives his definition ," A popular drama, on ITV or BBC, is one that gets the broadest audience and is, in terms of its production, as accomplished and as rigorous as possible."[282] He is damning of BBC policy on drama saying, " The BBC has alienated its populists. The real editorial infrastructure at the BBC is made up of people who want to make single drama and people who want to make prestigious high drama serials."[283] With this added to the BBC system of civil service bureaucracy, described by Jacey Lamerton as "ditherers", [284] it is perhaps no surprise that Neal's tenures at the BBC, though productive, have been relatively short. Particularly irritating must be the inability to find transmission dates for productions already completed.

---

[279] Ibid.

[280] The Bad and the Beautiful, Von Elstein to Jonathon Shields (Kirk Douglas), MGM, Vincente Minelli (dir.) (1952)

[281] Jacey Lamerton - Broadcast, 19.5.95.

[282] Ibid.

[283] Ibid.

[284] Ibid.

For instance *Bad Boy Blues,*[285] produced by Neal and directed by Andy Wilson in 1994 has been withheld subject to editorial processes. Wilson told me," *Bad Boys* they haven't shown for over a year because they're running scared of the violence in it, but its very realistic and it's based on a moral attitude. It's not pornographic violence therefore it's more disturbing than Arnold Schwarzenegger shooting a hundreds and sixty people in forty minutes. If you're not allowed to make stuff like that on television, then I don't want to work on television... I turn down television every week, even the Screen one and Screen two go through the corporate mill." [286] Presumably more of this caution before agreeing production and less after the event would save the licence payer thousands if not millions of pounds, and prevent the frustration and anger felt by those who have worked so hard on productions. Readers might remember that the original BBC production of Dennis Potter's *Brimstone and Treacle* suffered the same treatment before producer Kenith Trodd remade it as a feature in 1982.

Many would agree with Neal that the BBC operate a form of snobbery and that there is a hierarchy, particularly within the drama department. Chris Parr, producer of *Dangerfield* but perhaps better known for producing *Takin' Over The Asylum* and *Martin Chuzzlewit,* told Steve Clarke," I'm a late convert (to popular drama). The main problem is the culture within the BBC. Lots of us instinctively worked in singles and serials mainly because that was the culture. Series were something that other people did. In the end you barricaded yourself in."[287] Nick Elliott, who left LWT to become head of series at the BBC in Autumn 1994, also diagnosed a "cultural bias against mass audience drama"[288] during his uncongenial stay there. Described as "unlikely to walk out until he has secured a few hits under his belt,"[289] Elliott no doubt had suffered enough by the time he defected to the ITV Network Centre in April 1995, barely a month later. Ironically it was discontent with

[285]  *Bad Boy Blues* TX BBC2 1.6.96. Written by Biyi Bandele-Thomas
[286]  Authors interview, 30.11.95.
[287]  Broadcast, 24.3.95.
[288]  Broadcast, 19.5.95.
[289]  Broadcast, 24.3.95.

the BBC which allowed Neal to become controller of drama at Granada in June 1995. Sally Head vacated the post to become controller of drama at LWT, a job left unfilled since Sarah Wilson followed her predecessor , Nick Elliott, to the BBC at the end of 1994. [290]

Neal was determined to follow Head's example in the way she makes considered appointments and then supports her team in whatever way she can; in contrast to some executive producers at the BBC. I asked Andy Wilson if he had been better treated at Granada than at the BBC. "I'll say ! One hundred percent ! Sally is the shield and the cross, she's fucking brilliant ! As the executive producer she covered our arses like you wouldn't believe. Extraordinary !"[291] Describing *Cracker* as "a classic bit of Renaissance theatre," Neal qualifies it by saying "in the sense that you've got to fulfil certain expectations - you've got to tell a story - and if you can cram anything else in, whether it has any intellectual edge, that's great."[292] So it should be obvious that when looking for directors Neal searched for storytellers with a good track record but who could offer just that little bit extra. Knowing that the first episode would establish many supporting characters as well as setting the mood and tone of the series, Neal had to find someone with a facility for casting in addition to having visual style .

 His choice of **Michael Winterbottom** to direct the opening story perhaps betrays Neal's own background with both sharing a traditional classical education. After graduating in English from Oxford in 1982, Winterbottom went on to Bristol Polytechnic to take a Post-graduate course in Film and Television. He completed his studies by graduating with an M.A. from the Polytechnic of Central London in 1985 Winterbottom then joined Thames Television as an assistant editor, becoming an editor and doing some research before finally becoming a director in 1988. His early work won attention and acclaim, *Ingmar Bergman : The Director* winning Best Documentary at the Valladolid Film Festival and *The Strangers,* written by

---

[290]   Broadcast, 28.4.95.
[291]   Authors interview, 30.11.95.

Frank Cottrell Boyce, receiving a nomination for Best Educational film at the 1989 BAFTA. The film *Forget About Me* by the same author and shown on C4 in 1992 was selected for film festivals in London, Cologne and Lisbon in 1990 and 1991, and *Under The Sun* , written by Susan Campbell, selected for 1992 film festivals in London, Turin and Montreal. The work which preceded *Cracker* was *Love Lies Bleeding,* a BBC2 / Antenne 2 production written by Ronan Bennett, which won the Silver Medal at the New York Festival in 1993. Following *Cracker* , Winterbottom went on to direct *Family* , a BBC /RTE production which won the Writers Guild Award for Best Drama and the 'Pre-Europa" prize for Best Television Programme in Europe in 1994 and was nominated for a BAFTA as Best Series in 1995. *Butterfly Kiss* , another film written by Frank Cottrell Boyce, was also made in 1994, and in 1995 Winterbottom directed *Go Now* for the BBC, written by Paul Powell and Jimmy McGovern. *Go Now* was based on Powell's personal experience of multiple sclerosis. Winterbottom has just started production on a new film, *Sarajevo*, having finished *Jude,* a film produced by Andrew Eaton for Obscure Films. Winterbotton began his successful partnership with Eaton on *Family.*

,

With this list of accomplishments, Neal could be sure of a winner and could be certain of combining popularity with "an intellectual edge". Winterbottom is still modest despite his success; designer Chris Wilkinson described him as, "a nice lad from Blackburn"[293] Asked whether he had any influences or preconceptions about making *Cracker* Winterbottom said, " I just got on and shot it really." He attributes much of the success to the writing , finding that ,"the script had a lot of what you need to do in it. If you're doing a script about a serial killer, that already points you in a particular direction," then "you do what you think, do what feels best rather than having an over all strategy - I'm afraid," the last added as something of an apology. [294] In relationship to the script, he knew there were "loads of television series in the same area. I was conscious that Granada had done *Prime Suspect* and

---

[292]  Broadcast, 19.5.95.
[293]  Authors interview, 26.1.96.

aware of the fact that Sally had worked on that. It had been very successful and I wanted to make sure that it wasn't like that (*Prime Suspect*) but hoped it was going to be as successful. I didn't want it to be too similar." [295] He does admits that police procedural films like *Serpico* were of some influence in the way he approached *Cracker* but without the idea of "Let's shoot it all like this." He is an admirer of Scorsese's work and of other from the new wave of the mid-seventies. Winterbotton also likes sixties French films and German and Italian film of the seventies, but says he is not trying to imitate their style. Most important is "deciding what things should be like for a character; for example, in the police station what the light should be like, what sort of house made sense for Fitz as a character, how to light that. There was a certain amount of scruffiness and a lot of it was soft lit. I tried to make the camera movements naturalistic."[296] When he came to *Cracker*, two months before shooting commenced, it was already in its second draft. "The story was already there," Winterbottom told me, "I only added detail changes, changed the balance between characters." [297] However, in conversation and in his work, Winterbottom displays a deep understanding of his subject which I will illustrate when I come to discuss *Cracker* in depth.


Neal chose **Andy Wilson** to direct *To Say I Love You,* the second, and longest "Cracker" story in series one. Director and writer, Wilson studied drama at Birmingham University, graduating in 1979 and working as an actor for three years before establishing his own theatre company. He says," I started as an actor and acted in alternative theatre and the circus, I'm also a circus clown."[298] He directed fourteen major productions for the Rational Theatre and Hidden Grin, both on tour in the UK and Europe and at their base in London, the ICA in the period from 1980 - 1986, and began to write and direct for film and television in 1984. Early work, which he describes as

---

[294] Authors interview, 5.2.96.

[295] Ibid.

[296] Ibid.

[297] Ibid.

[298] Authors interview, 30.11.95.

"weirdo art films", included short films *Everything Under Control, The Job* shown on C4, which he both wrote and directed and *Shirts*. During the mid-eighties Wilson wrote *Fiddle City*, an adaptation of the Julian Barnes thriller for Working Title, and *Rococo*, based on the stage piece and commissioned for Derek Jarman also by Working Title. His experience in the theatre lead to further adaptations of stage work including *Bouinax In Love* which he directed as a pilot for a six part television series. It featured the French 'new circus' group Archaos with whom Wilson performed as a clown. An adaptation of *Anything For A Quiet Life* featuring the Theatre de Complicite, led to a C4 drama produced by Holmes Associates in 1989. *Dread Poets Society* , a BBC2 Screenplay written by David Stafford and Benjamin Zephaniah , was his next work as director , followed by the 1991 BBC2 series *The Mushroom Picker* adapted by Liane Aukin from the novel by Zinovy Zinik. In 1993, as Neal contracted him to direct *Cracker*, Wilson had his script *The Wolves* commissioned as a BBC Screenplay by executive producer George Faber. Wilson's direction led *To Say I Love You* to win the Golden Nymph at Monte Carlo Television in 1994 and the award for Best Director at the USA Cable Ace Award in 1995 Following his *Cracker* success, Wilson  directed *An Evening With Gary Lineker* which won  a Jury Commendation at the Prix Italia in 1994 and a BAFTA nomination for Best Single Drama in 1995. Since then, Wilson has shot *Bad Boys*, written by Biyi Bandele-Thomas and produced by Gub Neal for the BBC, although not shown   Wilson , whose work has also included pop promos, commercials and video installations, currently has "a raft of projects" in progress. He recently formed his own company to make commercials and has been raising finance for a feature  which he hopes to shoot in Hollywood later this year. In addition he has several writing projects underway, among them a treatment of Gormenghast for the BBC, a commission awarded by Gub Neal during his development period there. Wilson is also working on a project with J.G. Ballard who shares his views on television censorship. Ballard, Wilson tells me, feels that "what we need in this country is much more irresponsible television. I can't bear the responsibility of television in this country. What we need is more pornography and violence all over the screen.". What Ballard means, of course, is that debate always starts with pornography and violence. Wilson says, "the pornography of sexual relations aka human relations and violence the politics of human confrontation, that's the stuff of drama."[299] Wilson reminds me that he is "a moral person" and that "all drama should be morally uplifting ... I don't believe in gratuitous pornography and violence... Real drama is never representational ... its more dangerous and subversive. Television is supposed to anaesthetise the nation every evening so they don't go out on the streets and wonder what it's all about." Wilson and Ballard would seem be supporters of the radical dramatic movement that began to develop in Britain in the mid-sixties, McGovern is certainly a writer in that tradition. While sponsorship in America cut short new drama's life on television, in Britain it survived as *The Wednesday Play* Drawing on two major strands, the drama of internal dissolution (David Mercer's *In Two Minds*) and the drama of public action or public and private tension (Dennis Potter's *Nigel Barton* plays), it was a notable example of creative inspiration and exploration. John Hopkins quartet, *Talking to A Stranger*, explored alternating viewpoints, each play from the point of view of a different member of the family. There was also significant achievement in drama-documentary, for example, Jeremy Sandford's *Cathy Come Home*. Several of the most creative people got pushed to the margins because large audiences for controversial work caused embarrassment for the broadcasters. Raymond Williams notes that single plays, even when presented as a series, proved to be "difficult to arrange."[300] Now , of course, some of the creators of these "difficult" works are recognised as 'masters', allowing McGovern to receive the Dennis Potter Award.

Despite his alternative background and his strongly held views about the role of drama, the two films Wilson likes most, his "paradigm films", are classics; *Lawrence of Arabia* and *Doctor. Zhivago*, both directed by David

[299]   Ibid.

[300]   Television, Technology & Cultural Form. p.58

Lean.[301] Wilson says he has "watched *Lawrence of Arabia* a hundred times", even "in widescreen letterbox format on a 27" TV, it still looks great.... It's perfect." [302] Although he says, "It's a moral picture", a thing which is important to him, there is no doubt that it is the visual excellence of the films which impresses him most. Designer Chris Wilkinson found Wilson, "very design conscious", [303] and Wilson says of himself, "I'm much more of a visual artist than a literary artist. I come from a tradition of alternative theatre. Rational Theatre was called in the eighties a visual theatre company, which meant our expressed intention was to not allow the writing to dominate but make sure we always bore in mind the theatre was a visual medium. A person moving in an empty space is theatre. We worked with fine artists, top designers, made the visual aspect as important as the text. In fact sometimes there was no text. Television is a visual medium. Poor television is to do with economics mostly; its much easier ( and cheaper)[304] to shoot dialogue than to shoot big fuck off wide shots." Dramatic shots are important to Wilson who describes his style as "very theatrical" and "different to Michael". he says," I like to set up a shot and let the actors perform within a well composed wide shot. I don't use a lot of tracking, cutting, I tend to let the scene unfold." Wilson storyboards every shot allowing complicated work to progress quickly once on location. He cites as an example the scene in the bowling alley, which although originally only one page of dialogue, he felt needed seventy shots, completed in one day, to convey to the audience the impending dangerous situation which would erupt at the start of the following episode.[305] He got the confidence to begin storyboarding after reading about Martin Scorsese and seeing his storyboards. "I'm a better draw-er than him," he saying jokingly, "his figures are little stick men. But when you look at them you say that's exactly like the cutting." He admires this meticulous attention to detail and says it also impresses the crew, "they

---

[301] Lawrence of Arabia, Horizon (UK) 1962. Won seven Academy Awards including Best Picture and Best Director , Best Cinematography (Freddie Young) and three nominations. Doctor Zhivago, MGM, 1965. Won five Academy Awards including Best Cinematography (Freddie Young) and five nominations.

[302] Authors interview,30.11.95.

[303] Authors interview, 26.1.96.

[304] Authors addition in bracket

go, 'Oh, yeah, off we go, do all that'. I'm very insecure really and don't want anyone to say 'wanker' about me."[306] He puts his interest in visuals down to watching epic films at an "impressionable age", going to see *Bonnie and Clyde* and *2001* when they were released as well as his favourite Lean films. An interest in science fiction began early too with *Into The Unknown* and *Doctor Who* avidly watched on television at home. His interest in science fiction has stayed throughout his "career as a whacky alternative theatre director", and he lists the films of Tarkovsky as important as well as Bergman. Favourite is *The Sacrifice* which Wilson describes as "cheaply made and very personal yet extraordinarily defying and mysterious," he also likes *Stalker* which has a science fiction theme.[307] An interest in theatre came later and he says, "Jacobean tragedy is my favourite form of drama" but Wilson maintains wide and eclectic tastes. "As a kid, two programmes made an impression on me, *I Claudius*' and *Eyeless in Gaza* ... and I still like Robert Graves and Aldous Huxley." He became interested in film for its "potential to dream". He says, "you can visualise a dream of your own, then present it to other people and see if they can interface with your dreams. So on a subconscious level it's a very affirming art form. Its a much more dreamlike than theatre." It was this quality that attracted him to Tarkovsky and Bergman who always convey a very personal message.

It is important to Wilson that he is given freedom to treat a project in a personal way. He says, "Had I not liked the script of *Cracker* I wouldn't have done it. Gub sent me the script because he thought I would like it, and I did. ... Gub said 'do whatever you like with it, it's your piece, I'm not going to set a style, what I want is to let each director make it how they would like to... I read the first draft and thought there was a lot of crap in it but Jimmy was very quick to remove it. There weren't a lot of rewrites but I got a sprawling draft that would have been about four hours long. It was just a question of

---

305  To Say I Love You,sc.56.p.106.
306  Authors interview, 30.11.95.
307  The Sacrifice, Swedish Film Institute, Swedish TV, French Ministry of Culture etc. (Sweden & France)1986. Made the year before the Russian director Andrei Tarkovsky died of cancer. Filmed in Faro with a Swedish cast and crew, described as having a Bergmanesque quality. Stalker, Mosfilms (USSR) 1982. Shot in colour

emphasis and tightening. I told Gub I wanted to concentrate on the love story between Sean and Tina and shore that up, put some scenes in that show them having fun together so it's not all villain, villain, villain. I spoke to Jimmy through the medium of the script editor and a couple of times personally and he agreed, stripped the script out and we got on very well." Later he tells me, "I don't know what Jimmy thought of me. I think he thought I was over cavalier with the script. .. Jimmy is excessive. He's a genius. Full stop... He writes about what he feels, he's not a storyteller, he's a writer who needs organising...I think he was offended when I stripped the script. I don't collaborate with writers really." The real problem in fact seems to be the extra scenes Wilson asked for, Wilson cutting them in the edit when he found he did not need them after all. Although McGovern refrained from saying "I told you so" to Wilson, he has paraded his hurt by telling everyone else.

**Simon Cellan Jones** was the third director chosen for the first series of *Cracker.* He started in the industry as a mail boy at 20th Century Fox, a job he describes as "the one that came up. I was nineteen and need a job, I wasn't looking for the film business really." He adds, almost as an afterthought, "My Dad's a director. That might have something to do with it," and goes on to admit that , "the fact that he does that job has been an influence on me, but not his work, apart from a couple of exceptions. Some of the things he has done are very good. I did find that difficult, but I don't anymore. You get a lot of it at the BBC. (He is referring to following in his father's footsteps) I'm critical of people taking the easy route, but if you add it up, it helped. I didn't trade off it, but it's a noticeable name." Cellan Jones worked on "a couple of feature films as a runner" before joining the BBC where his first job was on *Edge of Darkness.* He worked as a location/production manager on BBC productions *A Perfect Spy* and *Blind Justice* and also spent three months in Beirut as a press photographer before completing the BBC directors course in 1989. Then he "sort of went off and borrowed some money and made my own film, started directing." His

and black & white, based on the novel  "Roadside Picnic"

film, *Looking After Number One*, was produced by Fat Boy Films as a BBC Screenplay and followed by directing assignments on *The Bill* and *Streetwise*, a TVS children's drama. Next Cellan Jones produced *City Shots* for BBC also directing one of the ten minute films, *The Missing Finger*. A stint on Granada's *Medics* was followed by BBC2 Screenplay, *Bitter Harvest* which was shot in the Dominican Republic in 1992. *The Riff Raff Element* , made in 1992/3, brought BAFTA success as Best Series in 1993 and Cellan Jones directed *Pig Boy* for the BBC before coming to *Cracker* also in 1993. Cellan Jones recently completed work on the BBC2 series *Our Friends In The North,* and has begun on a new BBC production.

Cellan Jones says he found *Edge Of Darkness* an "inspiration, before that I didn't know what they were." Talking of influence, he says he, "hasn't seen enough black and white films, but also haven't seen too many. Unlike some people" and describes *Midnight Cowboy* as his "favourite film." [308] He says he understands actors "a fair amount" because he understands "being frightened all the time, why they feel insecure." He says they can be "very challenging and suspicious people" but they "always give me an even break." He puts his success with performers down to paternal association, saying, "he (his father) is very good with actors ... I had an easier chance with a lot of them because they went, 'Oh, his Dad's OK so he probably is'." He describes himself as "very methodical, but then I change it all on the day. There's no point in planning too much because the buzz and excitement is what happens on the day, if you come in with prejudgments you're imposing something and not letting it breathe itself." He is, however, aware of the need for structure and says that although he made *Cracker* "as one piece ... for a screening," because "that's where you enjoy watching it most", he was aware of the need to plan for commercial breaks. He says, "In some ways having commercial breaks is good, it gives you a clear and formal three act structure, or whatever those script doctors call it... So I thought 'this is probably where a commercial break should be therefore this should be

---

[308]  UA, 1969. The only X-rated film to win an Oscar as Best Picture, it also won Academy Awards for John Schlesinger as Best Director, Waldo Salt for Best Adapted Screenplay and four Academy nominations including Dustin Hoffman as Best Actor.

slightly portentous and slightly dramatic to keep them waiting and hold them until after the washing up liquid adverts'.'" The way a piece is photographed is also important to him and although he did not "have much time to get conceptual over the way its lit", he always made time to supervise the operation of the camera. He says he does not mind using zoom lenses, even though cameramen tend not too, but prefers to use primes because it "creates a better discipline." He says, " I have only just started understanding about lenses so I'd use an 85mm whenever I could rather than a generalised version on a zoom. It makes me more disciplined too."

It was fortunate that Cellan Jones has a relaxed attitude and an "everyday approach" [309] to his work and that he found it "easy to collaborate with Jimmy," because the last *Cracker* story was not without production problems.

McGovern was brought in to rewrite *One Day A Lemming Will Fly* at a fairly late date, the original intention being for him write the first two stories, comprised of five episodes, and for another writer to end the series. Script editor Catriona McKenzie told me, "it's such a tall order to ask one writer to write as much as Jimmy has." Things did not go as planned however. Other writers, and McKenzie says, "believe me, we've been through so many," were "afraid of writing Fitz." She says, "It's not an executive question. They're frightened of writing Fitz because he's so much Jimmy and such an extraordinary character." McGovern admits, "There's an awful lot of me in him. At my worst I was Fitz at his worst, at his best he is the kind of person I aspired to be. At worst a gambler, boozer, smoker, at his best he's a man in pursuit of a pure motive, a kind compassionate man, but I'm rarely that." [310] I would have to disagree with the last, for in addition to being talented as a writer, McGovern is a most kind and compassionate man, in fact it is these qualities which make him a good writer. In view of the closeness of the originator to his character, it was difficult for any other writer to step into his

---

[309]  Chris Wilkinson, authors interview, 26.1.96.
[310]  Desert Islands Discs.

shoes, or indeed persona. McKenzie says, " The only person in the whole world we found who could write it was Paul Abbott who produced the second series." Abbott is better known as a writer than a producer, having written for *Coronation Street* for many years, he also won a BAFTA and a Writers Guild Nomination for the children's series *The Ward* which he co-created. Perhaps Abbott's proximity to *Cracker* while its producer gave him an advantage over other writers and allowed him to develop an empathy with Fitz, but this was not an option open during the creation of series one. Bringing McGovern in did not end all the problems because "he had to do it so fucking fast." [311] It is never clear whether Tim commits suicide after being beaten up and nearly strangled, or if, in fact, his attacker strings him up in a tree merely to disguise a successful strangling. Director Cellan Jones started shooting before the script was complete. McKenzie told me, "the ending changed about forty nine times," putting "the Fulford character through psychological convulsions which didn't quite gel."[312] The final script certainly shows evidence of several scenes being amended as late as the end of July, two days before filming began on 2nd August, and some even later, on the 10th of August, after filming had commenced.

Fortunate then, that Cellan Jones was able to take as his starting point "the difficulty and horror for the two parents," who were, "initially the stars for me. Although only for the first little while." He feels it is important for the drama to develop "from the people and the story" rather than to impose a style from outside. He had a lot of discussions where, "Me and Gub, but me and Jimmy mostly, talked about things we wanted," and then adapted to deal with personal understanding. He says, "you collaborate while you're doing it, but they don't say 'we want this' or they get told to fuck off ... Most directors get twitchy if you try and impose a style on them." He found Neal "definitely supportive" and thought he was "treated very well ... despite the relentless pressure." Describing Neal as "a very good producer," who does not play psychological games, the pressure was "always for a good reason," he also acknowledges Neal's part in *Cracker's* success. Although he says, "The

---

[311]   Catriona McKenzie, authors interview, 2.2.96.

two main reasons for *Cracker's* success were Jimmy McGovern and Robbie Coltrane, without question," he adds, "But Gub had a lot to do with it, he worked hard and put not a few ideas into it." [313] Cellan Jones expresses a great deal of admiration for McGovern and his writing, telling me, "I adore him. I think he's brilliant." He was attracted to Fitz because he's "not a sympathetic character and yet he is," because of all the weakness he has. He says that though it is common to have heroes with weaknesses he thinks, "Jimmy went to town on them and he was quite stubborn about wanting them to be there." Cellan Jones liked the idea of making Fitz wrong, although he "wanted him to be even more wrong, but we were so late getting the script.....". He goes on, "Television convention says that you have a hero as detective and you give him some weakness but he's always uncannily right. I was happy to undermine the idea. By the end of the series everyone knew that whenever Fitz said, 'Oh, have you looked in the wardrobe ?' there'd be something in the wardrobe so I wanted to undermine that and make him wrong."

Even so, Cellan Jones "nearly got what was wanted" when Fitz realises that the "ball he himself has set rolling now becomes the unstoppable machine of public and police desire for solution and retribution, which, bizarrely, the 'criminal' was quite happy to go along with - he embraced it." He says that kind of "lust for justice often gets in the way of truth. One often finds that justice and truth run on parallel lines." He compares it to the situation with the Guildford four or any terrorist attack, saying its like any murder case where children are involved, "you've got to get a conviction, whatever."

Truth and justice and the gap which often lies between are elements explored in many of McGovern's stories. He is particularly anxious to campaign for justice for anyone he sees as a victim of a system that has failed them, whether this is a failure of the law or giving someone a chance to put their views against those of a stronger protagonist. His need to find

---

[312]   Ibid.

[313]   Authors interview, 30.11.95.

justice, "real justice" for people unable to speak for themselves has led him to begin writing *Hillsborough*, a dramatisation of the Hillsborough football stadium tragedy. McGovern was angered by the treatment of the tragedy by the *Sun* newspaper and some of this shows in the *Cracker* story *To Be A Somebody* which started the second series. McGovern's need and ability to give a voice to those who have suffered loss or who cannot articulate for themselves, "disenfranchised people" as Andy Wilson [314] calls them, runs throughout his work, including *Cracker.*.

---

[314] Authors interview, 30.11.95.

# BIBLIOGRAPHY

## BOOKS

Alvaraelo, M. & J.O.Thompson (eds.), *The Media Reader, The Classic TV Detective Genre, Michael Westlake*, (London : BFI, 1990)

Axton, Marie & Raymond Williams, *English Drama - Forms and Development,* (Cambridge, London, New York, Melbourne : Cambridge University Press, 1977)

Belsey, Catherine, *The Subject of Tragedy - Identity & Difference in Renaissance Drama*, (London & New York : Methuen & Co. Ltd., 1985)

Cain, James M., *Double Indemnity and The Embezzler*, (London : Robert Hale Ltd., 1986)

------------------, *The Postman Always Rings Twice,* (Bath : Chivers Press, 1985)

Chandler, Raymond, *The Chandler Collection - Volume Three,* (London : Picador, Pan Books, 1984)

Copjec, Joan (ed.), *Shades of Noir*, (London & New York : Verso, 1993)

Crane, Rev. A. Bromley, *Facts of Faith*, (London : Burns & Oates, 1885, p.16-17)

Daalder, Joost (ed.), *The Changeling , Thomas Middleton & William Rowley*, (New Mermaids, London : A & C Black, New York : W W Norton, 1994)

Ellis-Fermor, Una, *The Jacobean Drama,* (London : University Paperbacks, Methuen & Co. Ltd. , 1973)

Gibbons, Brian (ed.), *The Revenger's Tragedy, Tourneur (?)* (New Mermaids, London : A & C Black, New York : W W Norton, 1994)

Kaplan, Ann (ed.), *Women In Film Noir,* (London : BFI, 1978)

Krutnik, Frank, *In A Lonely Street - film noir, genre, masculinity*, (London & New York : Routledge, 1991)

Lawrence, R.G. (ed.), *Jacobean & Caroline Tragedies*, (Everyman's University Library, London : J M Dent & Sons, 1974)

Luhr, William, *Raymond Chandler & Film*, (Tallahassee : The Florida State University Press, 1991)

Monaco, James & James Pallot & Baseline, *The Second Virgin Film Guide*, (London : Virgin Books, Virgin Publishing Ltd.,1993)

Murray, Peter B., *A Study of Cyril Tourneur*, (Philadelphia : University of Pennsylvania Press, 1964)

Parker, R.B. (ed.), *A Chaste Maid In Cheapside - Thomas Middleton,* (London : Methuen & Co. Ltd., 1969)

Piper, David, *The Illustrated History of Art*, (London : W H Smith Exclusive Books, Mitchell Beazley Publishers, 1991)

Ribner, Irving, *Jacobean Tragedy - The Quest For Moral Order,* (London : Methuen & Co. Ltd., 1962)

Schickel, Richard, *Double Indemnity,* (London : BFI, 1993)

Sparks, R., *Television and the Drama of Crime,* ( Open University Press, 1992)

Symonds, John Addington, (intro.) *Webster & Tourneur,* (London : The Mermaid Series, Ernest Bern Ltd., 1959)

Tuska, Jon, *Dark Cinema - American Film Noir in Cultural Perspective,* (Westport USA : Greenwood Press, 1984)

Williams, Raymond, *Modern Tragedy*, (London : Chatto & Windus, 1966)

-----------------------, (ed. Ederyn Williams), *Television, Technology & Cultural Form,* (London : Routledge, 1992)

-----------------------, (ed. Alan O'Connor), *Raymond Williams On Television - Selected Writings*, (London & New York : Routledge, 1989)

OTHER PUBLICATIONS

Clarke, Alan, *Television police series and the law and order,* (Unit 22 - Politics, ideology and popular culture, level 2) , The Open University Press)

*Press Packs, Cracker* - Series 1,2, & 3, (London : Granada LWT International Ltd., )

*Marketing Packs, Cracker* - Series 1, 2 & 3, (London : Granada LWT International Ltd.)

# ARTICLES - PERIODICALS & NEWSPAPERS

Barnard, Peter, 'Comic turns to crime', *The Times*, (28.9.93.)

Busfield, Steve, 'Head leaves Granada', *Broadcast*, (EMAP, 28.4.95., p. 7)

Broadbent, Lucy, 'Crackers about Coltrane', *Today*, (25.9.95.)

Bruton, Richard, 'Today's highlights', *The Telegraph*, (4.10.93.)

Butler, Robert, 'The man who raped Sheila Grant', *Independent On Sunday*, (5.2.95.)

Clarke, Steve, 'Dramatising the problems', *Broadcast*, (EMAP, 24.3.95., p.18.)

Driscoll, Rob, 'Cracker of a role', *Birmingham Evening Post*, (25.9.93.)

Dunkley, Christopher, 'Today's television', *Financial Times*, (8.11.93.)

Forwood, Margaret, 'Coltrane's cracked it', *Daily Express*, (2.10.93.)

Francis, Pam, 'Last night's view', *Today*, (28.9.93.)

Gibson, John, 'What a Cracker', *Edinburgh Evening News*, (28.9.93.)

Grant, Peter, 'Review', *Daily Post*, (8.11.93.)

----------------, 'Crime Cracker', *Liverpool Echo*, (27.9.93.)

Gritten, David, 'The taboo-breaker of television', *Daily Telegraph*, (2.2.95.)

Hebert, Hugh, 'Fitz and starts', *The Guardian*, (28.9.93.)

Keal, Graham, Coltrane promises us a real Cracker', *Northern Echo*, (23.9.93.)

------------------, 'Nuts about Crackers', *Liverpool Daily Post*, (1.10.93.)

Knight, Fiona, 'Robbie's quit drink to shrink', *Daily Record*, (11.10.93.)

Lamerton, Jacey, 'Neal diamonds' *Broadcast*, (EMAP, 19.5.95., p.18-19)

Leboff, Gary, 'Cracker is breath of fresh air', *The Sun*, (9.11.93.)

London, Simon, 'Big Rob takes the biscuit', *TV Daily Mirror*, (9.11.93.)

McKay, Ron, 'Coltrane waiting on platform', *Standard On Sunday*, (29.8.93.)

Middleton, Richard, 'Fitz adds a drop of fizz', *Daily Star*, (11.10.93.)

Middles, Mick, 'Cracker of a role for Coltrane', *Manchester Evening News*, (2.10.93.)

Miller, Compton, 'Coltrane's Cracker takes the biscuit', *Daily Express*, (28.9.93.)

Moore, Pat, 'Television review', *The Stage and Television Today*, (7.10.93.)

Norman, Barry, 'Why film noir is about a lot more than just fancy lighting and shadows', *Radio Times*, (14-20.10.95. p.58)

Norman, Matthew, 'Strong solution in a shrunken shrink', *The London Evening Standard*, (28.9.93.)

Ogden, John, *'Coltrane's the perfect choice'*, *Wolverhampton Express & Star*, (5.10.93.)

Ogle, Tina, 'Fitz and starts', *Time out*, (22.9.93.)

Paterson, Peter, 'Robbie it's a real cracker', *TV Mail Reviews*, (28.9.93.)

Paton, Maureen, 'Last night's TV', *Daily Express*, (5.10.93)

Penfold, Phil, 'Rob and roles', *Yorkshire On Sunday*, (26.9.93.)

Pickles, Anne, 'Big hero', *Yorkshire Evening Post*, (8.10.93.)

Sutcliffe, Thomas, 'Killer serial', *The Independent*, (28.9.92.)

Wright, Matthew & Karen Hockney & Jane Dimond, 'Don't miss this', *The Sun,* (4.10.93.)
Young, Graham, 'Big shrink', *Telly Mail,* (9.10.93.)

*Glasgow Daily Record,* (2.10.93.)
*Hello*, 'Pick of the week', (25.9.93.)
*New Statesman,* 'Review', (1.10.93.)
*Shropshire Star, 'Fitz of frustration',* (16.10.93.)
*TV Times,* 'In view',(25.9.93.)
*Yorkshire Evening Press*, 'Robbie tackles the psychology of crime', (27.9.93.)


## MANUSCRIPTS

McGovern, Jimmy, *Cracker - The Mad Woman In The Attic,* (Hour 1, final script, hour 2, final script, Manchester : Granada Television Ltd., 1993)

McGovern, Jimmy, *Cracker - To Say I Love You,* (Shooting script, issued 3.6.93.,Manchester : Granada Television Ltd., 1993)

McGovern, Jimmy, *Cracker - One Day A Lemming Will Fly,* (hour 6, final script, hour 7 final script, Manchester : Granada Television Ltd., 1993)


## UNPUBLISHED WORKS

Dunn, Josephine, *Hitchcock - In Search of a Proper Sense of Id-Entity*, M.A. essay, Derby University, 1994.

Dunn, Josephine, Cracker, M.A. essay, Derby University, 1994


## FILMS

*The Big Sleep,* (Howard Hawks, dir., Warner Brothers, 1946)

*Citizen Kane*, (Orson Welles, dir., Mercury, 1941)

*Double Indemnity,* (Billy Wilder, dir., Paramount, 1944)

*Force of Evil*, (Abraham Polonsky, dir., Enterprise, 1948)

*For Your Eyes Only,* (John Glen, dir., United Artists, 1981)

*In A Lonely Place*, (Nicholas Ray, dir., Santana, 1950)

*The Postman Always Rings Twice*, (Tay Garnett, dir., MGM, 1946)

TELEVISION & RADIO PROGRAMMES

*A Personal Journey With Martin Scorsese Through American Movies*, ( BFI, TX: C4, 21.5.95., 28.5.95., 4.6.95., 2030, 72mins. approx))

*The Changeling*, (TX : BBC2, 11.12.93.)

*Cracker : ep.1. - The Madwoman In The Attic*, (Michael Winterbottom,dir., Granada Television Ltd., TX : ITV, 27.9.93., 2100-2200)

*Cracker : ep 2. - The Mad Woman In The Attic*, (Michael Winterbottom, dir., Granada Television Ltd., TX : ITV, 4.1.93., 2100-2200)

*Cracker : ep.3. - To Say I Love You*, (Andy Wilson, dir., Granada Television Ltd., TX : ITV, 11.10.93., 2100-2200)

*Cracker : ep. 4. - To Say I Love You*, (Andy Wilson, dir., Granada Television Ltd., TX : ITV, 18.10.93., 2100-2200)

*Cracker : ep. 5. - To Say I Love You*, (Andy Wilson, dir., Granada Television Ltd., TX : ITV, 25.10.93. , 2100-2200)

*Cracker : ep. 6. - One Day A Lemming Will Fly*, (Simon Cellan Jones, dir., Granada Television Ltd., TX : ITV, 1.11.93., 2100-2200)

*Cracker : ep. 7. - One Day A Lemming Will Fly*, (Simon Cellan Jones, dir., Granada Television Ltd., TX : ITV, 8.11.93., 2100-2200)

*Cracker : The Mad Woman In The Attic*, (Michael Winterbottom, dir., Granada Television Ltd., TX : ITV, 26.3.94., 2100-2200 & 2230-2330)

*Desert Island Discs*, (Sue Lawley, pres., BBC, TX : BBC Radio 4, 14.1.96. , 0905-0945, RPT : 19.1. 96.)

*Gag Tag*, (BBC, TX : BBC1, 26.1.96., 1900-1930)

*Peter York's Eighties*, (BBC, TX : BBC2, 10.2.96., 2130-2200)

*Spiderman*, (on Live & Kicking, TX : BBC1, 10.2.96.)

*Twin Peaks*, (David Lynch, dir., TX : BBC2, 23.10.90. - Dec. 90. 8eps. & Jan.- June 91. 22eps.)

ADDITIONAL MATERIAL

Authors interviews :

Robbie Coltrane, Actor, (1985, 1986)
*Simon Cellan Jones*, Director, (30.11.96.)
*Jimmy McGovern*, Writer, (from April 1994 to February 1996)
*Catriona McKenzie*, Script editor / script associate, (20.4.94. and 2.2.96.)
*Craig McNeil, Production Executive* (Nov. 1995)
*Gub Neal*, Producer, (20.4.94.)
*Ivan Strasberg*, Cinematographer, (May & June 1994)
*Chris Wilkinson*, Production Designer, (26.1.96.)
*Andy Wilson*, Director, (30.11.95.)
*Michael Winterbottom*, Director, (5.2.96.)

Authors correspondence :

*Jimmy McGovern*, Writer, (from 1994 to 1996)

# ACKNOWLEDGEMENTS

I would like to thank:

Jimmy McGovern, without whom nothing would have been possible, and who has given much precious time and effort to help with this book.

Gub Neal, Catriona McKenzie, Michael Winterbottom, Andy Wilson, Simon Cellan Jones, Chris Wilkinson, Ivan Strasberg and Craig McNeil, who all gave interviews which have been invaluable.

Adrian Figgess, Sharon Leatham and Suzy Brown at Granada (Manchester) for providing manuscripts, press, marketing and other information

Mark Borkowski at Granada for press cuttings.

Leah Schmidt and Jo Armitage at The Agency.
Pauline Asper at Hamilton Asper Management.
Charlotte Kelly Management.
Catherine Hignett at Curtis Brown.
Town House Publicity.
Shelly Simmons (BBC publicity).
Sally in the Desert Island Discs office (BBC).
Yogita in the Broadcast & Research department at Granada LWT International.
Heather Thomas at ITV Global Entertainment (Clips Division).
Robb Hart, Producer & Director – responsible for the launch of MTV Europe

Information concerning the CRACKER television series provided by Granada Television Ltd.

Extracts from the scripts are by permission and are the copyright of Granada Television Ltd.

Screen Grabs of Cracker licenced in perpetuity worldwide for non-broadcast publication by "ITV Archive".

# ABOUT THE AUTHOR

Josephine Dunn was born in Melton Mowbray and brought up in Leicestershire and North Devon. She studied at Loughborough College of Art, graduated with a B.A. in Fashion Design & Communication from St Martin's College of Art and began working in television production at Southern TV / TVS. Later she worked at Limehouse Studios in London, then freelance in film and TV production before having a family and returning to the East Midlands. Having gained an M.A. in Film & TV Studies at Derby University, Josephine combined work in film, television and the media with teaching, bringing up her sons and renovating a crumbling Jacobean farmhouse. She is also published journalist and poet. Josephine has numerous credits in television[315] and has produced a number of short films including the award winning short feature *The Promise* (Large Scale Productions Ltd. Bronze Award Drama Worldfest Flagstaff, 1999). To view The Promise, visit https://www.youtube.com/watch?v=jyLWIKDv37g

---

[315] http://www.imdb.com/name/nm5158189/
http://ukscreen.com/josephined/

Printed in Great Britain
by Amazon

23527245R00088